THE WHOLE YOU

Creativity

THE WHOLE YOU

A GUIDE TO LIFE

Creativity

by Jeannie Kim

AN
APPLE
PAPERBACK

SCHOLASTIC INC.

NEW YORK TORONTO LONDON AUCKLAND SYDNEY
MEXICO CITY NEW DELHI HONG KONG BUENOS AIRES

Acknowledgments

This book was made possible by:

David Levithan, my creative inspiration, who saw a book in me before I saw it myself.

Fred Seibert, Parker Reilly, Anne Marie DeLuca, and all the kids at Secret Goldfish who shared their creative force, especially Amy, Chelsye, Courtney, and Marianne.

Izzy Rivers, who is one of the coolest kids I know.

My parents and my brother, who assume I can do anything.

And Adam. Of course.

ISBN 0-439-40462-2

12 11 10 9 8 7 6 5 4 3 2 1   2 3 4 5 6 7/0

Printed in the U.S.A.   40

First Scholastic printing, September 2002

Contents

Introduction
Find Your True Creativity

Welcome to **The Whole You!** In this, the first book in the series, you'll be unleashing your creativity and using it to discover the world and yourself. Get ready to create, play, adventure, and dream!

"But I'm not an artist!"

Think that CREATIVITY means being an Artist with a capital A? Think again. You don't have to be a great painter or a master musician to be creative. *Everyone* can have fun being creative, no matter what your talents or training might be. And everyone *should* be creative, because not only is it fun, it helps you grow and explore the inner you *and* the world around you.

> "Whoever undertakes to create soon finds himself engaged in creating himself."
> —Harold Rosenberg, art critic and author

Besides, in **The Whole You,** creativity doesn't mean simply artistic expression — it also includes curiosity, adventure, and dreaming big. All of those things, as well as more typically "artsy" activities, are creative because they help you create your own vision of life

1

and let you express your inner self to the outside world. **Anything you do that teaches you about yourself is creative, because it helps you create *you*.** In fact, **The Whole You** itself is a creative project!

What is The Whole You?

Right now, a whole world of options is opening up around you. Whether you know it or not, your life is full of amazing opportunities, and you yourself are overflowing with all kinds of potential and personality and talent that you've only just begun to discover. **The Whole You** is based on the idea that it's important to explore all of those options, **to grab every chance to learn something new about the incredible, exciting whole that is you.**

Why is this important? **The more you know about yourself, the easier it will be to make the right choices about your life** — choices that keep you whole and happy instead of making you feel like you're torn apart.

Since **The Whole You** is about discovering YOU, you get to decide the path you take. That means I won't be giving you a bossy set of instructions on the best way to live your life or a boring list of ten steps to success. You're creating *yourself* — there's no magic formula for that. I'll also never tell you that there are a million things wrong with you that you need to fix. That's because every single person who reads **The Whole You** is different, and cool in her or his own way.

I'm not a teacher or a psychologist. But as a writer and editor for teen magazines, I've spent tons of time talking to kids from all over the world about the stuff that matters most to them. And of course, I've also been through a lot of the same kinds of struggles, questions, good times, and bad times that you're going through right now. So throughout **The Whole You,** I'll share stories from my own experiences, as well as those of other kids. (You'll see those marked with a ✓ "REALITY CHECK".) Everything in **The Whole You** is based on real life — not on some theory about how kids are supposed to be.

Finally, and most important, **The Whole You** is supposed to be fun. You'll find plenty of hands-on activities to get you thinking and playing — and, I hope, excited about exploring the whole you!

How to use this book

Like I said before, **The Whole You** is *your* journey —
so you're the one who decides the way you want to use
it. Every chapter of **The Whole You** is packed with
activities and exercises. There are ***WRITE IT!***
exercises you can do right in the book or in a separate
notebook. ***WORK IT!*** activities are more hands-on;
you might find it fun to do some of them with friends.

These activities are very important in this book,
since the whole point of a book on creativity is to get
you to do stuff *outside* these pages. Think of this book
as a workbook that you can use as a launching pad for
creative fun. My goal is for you to scribble in it, dog-
ear it, drip paint and clay and glue on it, and carry it
around so much that it gets battered beyond recogni-
tion!

You don't have to do every single activity — just
do the ones that appeal to you and save the rest for
later. You don't have to start reading at the beginning
of the book and work straight through to the end,
either. (Creativity definitely doesn't happen in a
straight, orderly line.) In fact, I encourage you to skip
around — to help you do that, I've included **LINKS** ✂
in each chapter to point you to other chapters, other

books in **The Whole You**, even Web sites and other resources that might interest you. You might feel like skimming through one chapter, then spending hours on another chapter, doing every single activity — it's up to you.

A special note on creativity and perfectionism

Ever hear that saying, "If you can't do something right, don't do it at all"? Forget about it. That's perfectionism talking, and for all of **The Whole You**, it's important to try to let go of any perfectionist tendencies you might have — that means *no* worrying about whether you're doing something "right." As a perfectionist myself, I know firsthand that putting pressure on yourself to do everything perfectly the first time can be a real creativity killer. If you don't allow yourself to mess up once in a while, you're a lot less likely to experiment or play around, which is where a lot of great creativity comes from.

So don't worry if you never thought you could be a good painter or writer. No one has to see or know about any of the activities you do in this book. There's no right or wrong way to do any of them. Even if you think you stink at an activity, as long as it's fun, you're getting something out of it.

To loosen up when I have writer's block, I always tell myself "It's okay if the first draft stinks." By giving myself permission to write something that might not be so great, I remove the pressure of having to get it perfect right away. So to warm up for this book, I suggest you do the same: Stand in front of a mirror, look yourself in the eye, take a deep breath, and say loudly, **"I hereby give myself permission to stink!"**

Ready? Now check out a fun activity. Dive into a project. And uncover the creative you!

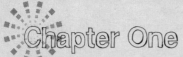

Chapter One
Discover Your Inner Artist

Be artsy!

For most of us, the word *creativity* brings to mind what we think of as "the arts" — things like painting, writing, music, and dance. Maybe you love doing that stuff, or maybe you've never tried it. The point of this book is that *everyone* can be artistically creative, even if you don't think of yourself as a talented artist. One of the great things about creativity is that there really isn't a wrong way to be creative.

The arts are also great for your brain and general peace of mind. Expressing your feelings artistically helps you understand and share them, as well as helping you release stress and making you generally happier. Taking pride in something you create feels good and strengthens your sense of self. The arts also work lots of mental and physical muscles, keeping you flexible and giving you new strengths

✛○*LINKS*
See *Spirit*, Chapter 3 (The Way You Feel), for more on your feelings and how to handle them. *Spirit*, Chapter 5 (Accepting Yourself — and Everyone Else), also talks about taking pride in your accomplishments.

that you can apply to all areas of your life. And most important, they're fun!

In the next few chapters, we'll talk about different ways to be creative: visual arts, performing arts, writing, and other creativities. Go ahead and sample something from every chapter, even if you've never tried, say, sculpting anything before. You don't have to be an artistic genius or even be all that good at it. There's no right or wrong way to do any of the activities in this book. Just plunge in and enjoy!

Envisioning the arts

The *visual arts* are usually what people think about when they hear the word *art*. The term includes familiar things like drawing, painting, and sculpture but also areas like design, fashion, and photography.

✔ ***REALITY CHECK*** "I don't think I'm good at art, but I create some sweet collages," says Amy. "I can construct a collage in about an hour — sometimes they're just random pictures and things, and sometimes they have themes. I've made collages of pictures of my family, gum wrappers, pictures of cars, and even beach collages. They're fun for me to do, and the two hours or so it takes for me to do them lets me stop thinking and just create. It gives me an outlet and really lets me kind of escape."

"When I was little, I would sit on the floor with a stack of paper and a pair of scissors and just cut out designs for hours," remembers Marianne. These days her love of art has expanded to include origami, calligraphy, digital art and Web design, and decorating her room.

Courtney expresses her love of visual arts on a stage crew. "It's woodworking and drawing put together," she explains. "I love to design sets and to draw. Those things keep me sane. When I'm designing or building, all my problems go away."

The visual arts focus, obviously, on *vision* — the vision you have of the world around you, and the vision you have inside of the way you'd like to see the world. So the first thing I'd like you to do is to really focus on the things you see around you. Fill yourself up with vision.

> "Art does not reproduce the visible; rather, it makes visible."
> — Paul Klee, painter

9

✳*WORK IT!* WARMING UP: Pick a place you find visually appealing or interesting. It could be a busy street corner, a park bench next to a pond, a view of a snowy yard, a beautiful garden. Spend a minimum of ten minutes there just soaking in the sights. Don't try to draw or paint or photograph it — just fill your brain with everything you see. Notice the **colors** — are they bright, muted, harsh, faded, happy, soothing? What kind of **shapes** do you see — smooth, jagged, angular, rounded, large, tiny? Look at the **textures**, too — do things look soft, hard, shiny, rough, mushy, prickly? What about the **light** — is it bright, dim, harsh, soft, dappled, tinted with color?

Why do you need to fill up like this? Any creative activity involves pouring out a part of yourself into the world, whether it's painting a picture of something you see or wish you could see, writing about an experience you had, or playing a piece of music. So it's important to recharge your batteries with fresh energy, whether that means absorbing a beautiful or interesting scene like in the activity above, listening to a great song, or just living your life to the fullest.

Playing with art

A lot of us are intimidated by the visual arts. Once we get old enough to get grades in art class, we sometimes believe that you have to be good at drawing to attempt anything visual. But remember, creativity here is all about play. When you were a little kid, you probably drew and painted and rearranged your world all the time, because it was fun. You didn't care if what you drew looked exactly like real life, and you didn't care if you made a mess while you did it. That fearlessness and fun are crucial to unleashing your creative energy. So in the spirit of kindergarten, play around with these activities:

> ❀*LINKS*
> Turn to Chapter 5 (Curiosity Counts) to learn about how your natural curiosity can help fill you up. Read more about replenishing your soul in *Spirit,* Chapter 6 (Peace Out!).

✳*WORK IT!* Get a set of finger paints (the kind little kids use) or little-kid fat crayons or markers. Use your nondominant hand to create a picture — if you're right-handed, use your left, and vice versa. It doesn't matter what you draw or paint — if you want, just make washes and splotches of color on the page. The point of using your nondominant hand is to release yourself from the responsibility of drawing something recognizable — you can't control the hand, anyway, so let go a little. If you still find yourself trying really hard to draw something "good," put the paper on the floor and use your feet!

☀*WORK IT!* Still have that Play-Doh from when you were little? Dig it out, or make your own: Mix together two parts flour, one part salt, a tablespoon or two of vegetable oil, and enough water to make it all stick together in a claylike consistency. Add food coloring if you want. (Be careful with the food coloring, since it can stain carpets, clothes, and even hands!) Take your Play-Doh or homemade clay and use it to make a sculpture of yourself or someone you know.

☀*WORK IT!* Get an ink pad (the kind you use with rubber stamps) in any color, or pull out those finger paints again. Ink up your whole hand and use it to stamp a sheet of paper. What does the shape/color/texture remind you of? Create a design using only inky impressions of your own body parts — hands, feet, elbows, even your belly or your face. Make a mess! (Just make sure that the ink washes off with soap and water before you spread it all over your body!)

Now that you've warmed up, here are some more activities to try:

☀*WORK IT!* Go nuts with pencil rubbing. Collect some flat objects with interesting textures — coins, rough fabrics, bumpy pieces of wood, corrugated cardboard, a cool plate, a leaf. Place your object on a table and hold a sheet of paper on top of it. Rub a soft pencil lightly over where the object is until an impression of it appears on the paper. Try using different colors of pencils or crayons and different kinds of paper for different effects. You can do this with bigger stuff, too — a brick wall, a license plate, a tree trunk. Just lightly tape the paper in place so it doesn't slip.

WORK IT! Make your own stained glass window. Get a sheet of tracing paper or vellum (a fancy semi-sheer paper sold in art stores). Draw or trace a design on it. Outline your design in heavy black marker, and fill it in with brilliant colors. You can fill in the whole sheet, or just trace a shape and cut the shape out when you're done. Tape your work of art to a sunny window and admire the view.

WORK IT! Create a mosaic. Glue bottle caps, seeds, dried beans, pebbles, or all of the above onto a piece of cardboard to create a cool design. If you want to, you can paint the pieces, either before or after you glue them down. For a cool psychedelic effect, paint bunches of pebbles (or whatever you're using) different colors. When dry, pour them carefully onto your sheet of cardboard and stir them around with your finger to mix them up into an interesting pattern. Glue them down exactly where they are.

✹ *WORK IT!* Put together a photo collage. Dig out a bunch of old photos, or grab a camera and shoot a couple of new rolls. They can be pictures of your friends, pets, cool street signs, anything you like. Put them together in a collage — cut them up, mix them up in weird combinations, add captions or decorations if you want.

✹ *WORK IT!* Fill this space with art. Do anything you want — draw, paint, make a collage, doodle designs, anything that feels fun to you.

Visualizing what's inside

For thousands of years, people have used the arts, especially the visual arts, to express their feelings about things that happen to them. Little kids don't always know the words to talk about their feelings or the way they see the world, but psychologists use the pictures children draw to help understand their feelings. The same goes for those of us who are a little older: Our artistic expressions can communicate things we might not always have the words for, whether that means stressful emotions or deeply personal parts of ourselves. Ultimately, looking inside with an artistic eye can help you visualize the whole you better.

> **"Painting is a blind man's profession. He paints not what he sees, but what he feels, what he tells himself about what he has seen."**
> **— Pablo Picasso, artist**

☼*LINKS* Go to *Spirit,* Chapter 3 (The Way You Feel), for more about all your different emotions.

✷*WORK IT!* Pick an emotion, like joy, sadness, fear, anger, love. What colors go with that emotion to you? Using those colors, create an image (by drawing, painting, sculpting, collage, or anything) that expresses that emotion to you.

✱"WORK IT!" Create an image (or set of images) or sculpture of the inside of your mind. Think of a unique way that you can express your unique self. Here are some ideas you could try:

- Make a collage of thoughts, words, and images that might run through your brain.
- Draw the shape of an actual brain — don't worry too much if it's not exactly realistic. Divide it into sections according to what's important to you, and label and color code it as if it's an anatomy chart showing the parts of the brain. For example, if soccer rules your brain most of the time, you might color in a huge section right at the front and label it "soccer." If you avoid cleaning your room as much as possible, you might blacken a tiny part on the underside of the brain and label it "cleaning."
- Fill a shoe box or large egg carton with items that represent pieces of your personality.

❖*LINKS*
See *Spirit*,
Chapters 1
("Who Am I?")
and 2 (What
Matters to
You — and Why
It Matters), for
inspiration on
what to include
in your mental
images.

- Make a photo gallery or album of photographs taken from your life.
- Imagine what your mind would look like if it were an actual space. Would it be a cozy bedroom? A peaceful meadow? A crazy toy store? What would be in it? What colors would it be? Draw, paint, sculpt, or collage it. (To "sculpt" a space, you could try making a little shoebox model, like a dollhouse.)

WORK IT! Think of a memorable moment you've had recently. Was it happy? Sad? Embarrassing? Create an image portraying what happened. Use images to show how you felt. (For example, if you were really proud or excited, you might show yourself flying through the air.)

A bigger brain through art

One of the great things about creative activities is that they teach you to use your brain in different ways. In school, you probably use your brain in a very analytical way, focusing on words and numbers. The visual arts help stimulate the parts of your brain that deal with space and shapes, ways of seeing, and other areas of your mind that might not get a lot of attention otherwise. This helps you to use your whole brain more, and the more of your brain you exercise, the more you can tap into all your creative and personal potential. Try these brain-stretching activities:

> **❖*LINKS***
> **Check out** *Body and Mind,* **Chapter 4 (Feed Your Brain), for more activities that will give your brain a workout**

✸*WORK IT!* Find a picture you like — it could be a photograph of you and a friend, a picture of a car or a house you like, even a page ripped out of a catalog. Now, using a pencil and paper, copy the picture as best you can. But here's the catch: Turn the picture upside down, and copy it that way. The idea here is that by drawing the picture upside down, instead of just trying to draw a nose or a flower or a wheel, you'll concentrate on the shapes and lines in the picture, drawing those instead.

✸*WORK IT!* Make a shape collage. Cut out pictures of flowers from magazines and glue them to a sheet of paper in the shape of a flower; or choose another image, whether it's computers, books, shoes, or suns. If you're feeling really ambitious, use the colors of each picture to help shape your image — for example, you could use darker-colored flower pictures for the center of your flower shape, and brighter-colored ones for the petals.

WORK IT! Draw your hand — without looking at what you're drawing. Here's how: Tape a piece of paper to your desk or table, and hold the tip of your pencil to the paper. Then turn your body away so you can't see the paper, and focus on your other hand. Look at this hand very carefully and intensely as you draw it — again, without looking at what you're drawing. It doesn't matter if what you draw ends up looking nothing like your hand. Just go really slowly, and think carefully about the outline that you're drawing.

WORK IT! Make a puzzle. Take a favorite photo and enlarge it using a computer or color copier, or create a large picture or painting of your own. Glue the image to a same-sized piece of cardboard, making sure to coat every bit of the back of the image with glue. (You could also paint or draw directly on the cardboard.) When the glue is dry, cut the cardboard into randomly shaped pieces. If you want to get really fancy, you can keep the pieces in a box or bag with a smaller copy of the picture attached.

The art in every day

The visual arts appear in many aspects of our lives, from the colors on the cover of this book to the shape of a computer. There's amazing artistic potential in your whole world, once you open your eyes to all the possibilities. Everyday objects, like spoons and bookshelves, can be artistically beautiful in their own right. We can add joy to our everyday lives by taking pleasure in the beauty of things around us and by trying to add visually pleasing things to all areas of our lives.

✳*WORK IT!* Pretend you're from another planet, and you can't tell the difference between humans' "art" and "useful" objects. Carry a camera around for a day, and take pictures of anything that strikes you as visually or artistically

✂*LINKS*

New York's Museum of Modern Art maintains architecture and design collections dedicated to buildings, objects from appliances to cars, and examples of graphic design like posters and type. You can check out photos of items from the collection at *http://www.moma.org/*.

interesting. What everyday things are beautiful to you? Some examples: a kitchen appliance, a cell phone, a leaf, a glass, a billboard, a train track, a hat. When you get the photos developed, pick a few that look especially interesting and frame them as if they're works of art. (No need to buy a fancy frame — you can make your own by cutting a piece of cardboard to the right size and decorating it as you like.)

☀*WORK IT!* Make a decorative border for this page. That's right, do it right in the book. Draw, stamp, use stickers and stars, sketch designs or faces, whatever you feel like. If you've got more than one idea, decorate more than one page.

☀*WORK IT!* Pick your favorite book. Design a new cover for the book. What colors would you use? What kinds of images, if any? What kind of typefaces (fonts) would you use for the title and author's name?

22

☀️*WORK IT!* Design a poster for your favorite movie. How would you advertise it? What kinds of images would you use?

☀️*WORK IT!* Turn an everyday object into a work of art. Pick something of yours that's relatively plain — a mirror, a brown paper-bag textbook cover, a pair of jeans, a cell phone case, your desktop. Decorate it with paints, glitter, glued-on objects (like shells or buttons), stickers, fancy edging made of cardboard, ribbons, sequins, photos you love, pictures cut from magazines — anything you like. (Just ask permission first, and be sure not to decorate your object so much that it becomes unusable — like, don't glue macaroni all over your jeans!)

☀️*WORK IT!* Pick a corner of your room to redecorate. (If you want, you can go for the whole thing, but we'll start with just a corner to make it easier.) Designate that area as your sanctuary. To start, select colors you love. Drape a chair (or whatever other furniture goes

23

there, like your desk) with fabric in that color. (Think of other cool ways to incorporate your favorite colors — can you paint the walls or hang posters or framed pictures in those colors?) Fill the area with objects that are beautiful to you. Make sure to include pillows, beanbags, or something else to flop on.

What else can you do to decorate? Can you separate the corner from the rest of the room by hanging up a curtain? (One cool curtain idea: String old CDs you don't want on fishing line by running the cord through the center hole and knotting at the edge, so the CD is held in place by a loop. Hang lots of strings from the ceiling for a space-agey effect.) How about sticking photos on the walls to cover every inch of space? Experiment. If you love what you've done, do it to the rest of your room. (Again, ask permission before you paint, glue, or pound nails into your walls!)

> **✂ *LINKS***
> **For more cool art activities and resources, flip to Appendix A (Books to Indulge Your Creativity).**

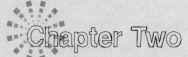

Chapter Two
Performing the Arts

Showing off the whole you

✓ **"REALITY CHECK"** Heather loves taking in the performing arts, whether it's listening to music or seeing a Broadway play. Chelsye gets into performing in plays at school and writing and performing songs for her band.

Marianne plays oboe and has started to get into theater, too. "I don't think of myself as an actress, but I love the way I can just forget my worries and be silly onstage," she says.

You may not think of yourself as a performer, but the performing arts are still something everyone can do and enjoy. Music, dance, theater, and film (which combines several performing arts with the visual arts) are all ways that you can work through many of the different emotions and ideas that make up the whole you. Like other creative activities, the performing arts also help to rejuvenate the whole you and fill you up with

❖*LINKS*
The performing arts are too huge to cover in just one book, let alone one chapter, so try checking out some of the books in Appendix A (Books to Indulge Your Creativity), too.

new energy and emotions, whether you're a participant or part of the audience.

In this chapter, we'll talk about different ways you can explore the performing arts, without ever having to get on a stage.

Music

Music surrounds us from day one, from the lullabies people sing to us as babies to the songs we listen to on the radio to the rhythm of our own heartbeats. Whether or not you think of yourself as musical, music is part of the fabric of your whole life. It's also one of our most basic art forms: From the time that our ancestors tapped out simple beats on early drums or even on their own bodies, music has been a way to express ourselves.

Music is one of the hardest art forms to write or talk about. Ever tried to describe a song to someone without singing it? I think that's because it's also one of the most visceral, or gut-connecting, art forms. Music connects to your body and emotions in a very direct way. Unlike writing, for example, you don't have to think about music or have any special skills (like knowing the alphabet) to appreciate it. If you *do* know a lot about music, you can enjoy the complicated, wonderful world of notes, scales, structure, and lyrics. But if you don't know anything about music, you can still lose yourself in the beauty and power of sound and rhythm. At its most basic, music bypasses the brain and goes directly to your heart, making you feel uplifted, sad, jumpy. Even if you can't see or hear, you can understand the feeling of a rhythm.

> "After silence, that which comes nearest to expressing the inexpressible is music."
> — Aldous Huxley, author

In that spirit, then, we'll be focusing on that gut-connecting part of music — that indefinable thing that makes you want to get up and dance, or sit and be quiet, or hug your friends and tell them you love them. The activities in this section are designed so that you can have fun with them whether you're a musician or not.

✳ **"WORK IT!"** WARMING UP: Find a comfortable place to sit or lounge with a radio nearby. Scan through the stations and randomly pick a few that are playing different kinds of music: classical (loud, mellow, happy, dramatic), pop (sappy love songs, upbeat sing-alongs), rock, country, hip-hop, polka, dance, show tunes, or anything else your local radio stations offer. Explore some stations you don't ordinarily listen to. Spend a few minutes on each one, listening and absorbing the music only — try not to pay attention to the words, if there are any. Close your eyes, if that helps you listen better. How does each piece of music make you feel? Is there more than one mood or feeling to it?

Connecting to the rhythm

Rhythm is the backbone of music, its heartbeat. Rhythm in music is what makes you want to get up and dance or makes you feel slow and draggy. But music isn't the only thing that depends on rhythm — it's built into our whole lives. There's a rhythm to everything we do, from the daily beat of get-up-go-to-school-come-home-go-to-bed to the steady *ba-bum* of your heart. Speech

✂️*LINKS*
For more on how rhythm can move you, be sure to check out the section on dance, which follows.

has a rhythm, and so does skipping, and soccer, and snoring. Traffic, rain, typing, stirring a pot, a ringing phone — all of those things create rhythms, regular and irregular, that surround you every day.

☀ *WORK IT!* Find a comfortable place to sit or lie down — it can be inside or outside. Close your eyes, and listen to the sounds around you. What kinds of rhythms do you hear? (As I write this, I hear the rushing sound of traffic stopping and starting outside my apartment window; the honking of horns every once in a while; the rumble of a bus; children shouting and laughing; my window shades rattling and banging back and forth in the breeze; the creak of my desk chair as I shift positions.) Try this in a different location, standing still. What rhythms do you hear in your backyard, in a quiet room, by a busy street, in a crowded cafeteria?

◗ *WRITE IT!* What are your favorite everyday sounds? (Some of my favorites are the sound of rain on the window during a thunderstorm, the way my cat purrs when she's happy, and the clatter of my computer keyboard when I've got a great idea and can't stop typing.) List five of your favorites.

_____

_____

_____

_____

_____

⚡"WRITE IT!" For one day, listen for sounds or rhythms that are striking, unusual, or just interesting to you, and make a note of them (some examples: the squeak-squeak of chalk on the chalkboard, the clanging of dishes and trays in the cafeteria, the thud of a can dropping out of the soda machine, the rustling of papers during a test, the screeching sound the school bus door makes when it opens, the snuffling of your dog as he settles down to sleep). Have a friend make a list of notable sounds, too, and compare your lists.

✳"WORK IT!" Create your own rhythm makers and try out different kinds of sounds and rhythms. Try some of the ideas below, or invent your own instruments:

- **Drums:** Decorate an empty coffee can (the kind with a plastic lid) to make a handheld bongo. Experiment with different sizes and shapes of containers — a big Tupperware container, a cardboard box, a metal canister, an upside-down garbage can. Try different ways of hitting your drums — on top, along the edges, on the sides, with your hands, chopsticks, wooden spoons, pens, pillows. If you can take the lid off your container, try replacing the lid with different materials, like a piece of fabric or waxed paper stretched tight over the opening (use rubber bands or tape to secure it in place). Pay attention to the different kinds of sounds you can make.
- **Cymbals:** Experiment with different sizes of metal pot lids or garbage can lids (moms love this — not!). Listen to the different sounds when you bang them together, tap them with sticks, flick them with your finger, or plop them on the floor.

✂️*LINKS*
In the show STOMP, performers use everyday objects like brooms, pipes, garbage cans, and matchbooks to create complex rhythms that they incorporate into a dance/theater performance. You can learn more about it and try some activities they've developed to teach students about rhythm and the science of sound at http://www. stomponline. com/percuss1. html.

- **Maracas:** Fill a small jar or box about one-quarter full with dried beans, beads, or little pebbles. Put the lid on, and tape it shut if necessary. Decorate it, and shake it around to your own beat. Try using different amounts of filler, and see how it sounds. Or try different containers, like a toilet paper tube with paper taped over each end. (You can pour some filler into your drum, too, for another kind of sound.)

- **Your body:** Your body can be an incredibly versatile rhythm maker. Try drumming on your stomach or chest, puffing out your cheeks and flicking them with your fingers, rubbing your hands together, clapping, stomping, slapping your legs, making swishing or clicking sounds with your mouth . . . the possibilities are endless.

✳️*WORK IT!* Pick a piece of music, any style. Play it on your stereo or radio, and using one or more of your homemade rhythm makers, add your own rhythms and beats to the music.

Feeling the music

Music is so personal that any time you create it, you're expressing a bit of the whole you, either through the music itself (like an elegant melody or a weird, dissonant harmony) or the way you produce it (like playing a drumbeat really aggressively, or deciding to put a sad, quiet song right after a loud, angry song on a mixed tape).

✄ *LINKS*
For more on expressing and coping with emotions, turn to *Spirit*, Chapter 3 (The Way You Feel), and *Body and Mind*, Chapter 5 (Feeling Healthy).

As I said earlier, music connects with your feelings in a very direct way. So it's natural to use music to help yourself work through or express emotions.

Music has been an emotional outlet for me for a long time. I started playing the violin when I was four, so I can't remember a time when it wasn't a part of my life. Whether I was playing in an orchestra in high school and college or, later, playing in a rock band, I could head to rehearsal or practice in the foulest, nastiest mood possible and emerge at the end feeling tired but excited and wiped clean of all the nastiness.

> **"Good music stirs by its mysterious resemblance to the objects and feelings which motivated it."**
> — Jean Cocteau, author and filmmaker

Not everyone is a musician, of course, but you don't have to play an instrument or even be able to sing in tune to express yourself through music. Sometimes simply dancing around — or punching pillows — to the right tune can crystallize what you're feeling. Music can also help you explore and experience feelings you've never felt before. It can lift you up, bring you down, or create any other kind of mood change you want.

✸ ***WORK IT!*** Head for your room or another private place. If you don't have a radio or CD player in there, bring one with you. Pick out music to play as loud as you can stand. (It's good to do this activity when no one else is home or at least to warn everyone else that you're doing it.) It doesn't matter what kind of music it is — pop, rock, or classical; happy, sad, or angry — as long as it fits your current mood and sounds good loud. How do you feel when the music is over? Did it make you happier, sadder, angrier? If you were in a bad mood when the music started, did it help you vent your yucky feelings, or did it make it worse?

"WORK IT!" In the previous exercise, you picked music to go along with your mood. Now do the opposite: Pick music to *create* a mood. Find the right music to fit the mood you want to explore — the perfect writing-in-your-journal-with-the-lights-turned-low music, for example, or the quintessential getting-ready-for-a-party music. There's also cheer-up-when-you're-feeling-down music, mellow-out-when-you're-too-wound-up music (good for stressful days and for when you're pulling baby-sitting duty), get-silly-to-take-your-mind-off-things music — can you think of more?

"WRITE IT!" Make a list of your 10 favorite songs or pieces of music. What moods do you associate with them?

Song or piece	Mood(s)
1. _____	_____
2. _____	_____
3. _____	_____
4. _____	_____
5. _____	_____
6. _____	_____
7. _____	_____
8. _____	_____
9. _____	_____
10. _____	_____

Creating music

Okay, so maybe you don't play an instrument and you'd never sing in public. But if you tried some of the rhythm activities, you've already made music. Try these, too:

✳"WORK IT!" Put on a recording of a song you know really well, whether it's a pop song, a show tune, or an operatic aria. Hum or sing along, and try to come up with your own part or harmony. It could be really simple, like singing the melody line a beat behind the singer or going "ooh" at the start of every line, or it could be more complicated, like a new harmony. Don't worry if it sounds weird or you hate your voice — no one's listening, right?

✳"WORK IT!" Make a mixed tape or CD. Okay, technically you're not making the music itself, but by putting different songs together in a unique combination, you're creating a musical experience that no one else has ever made before. To help guide you, think about the mood you want to create with the music, and who it's for (yourself? a friend?). Pay attention to how the songs work together. Here are some examples of themes you can use as a guide:

- A nostalgic mix: Choose songs that remind you of camp or of the past school year.
- A friendship mix: As a gift to a friend, pick out friendship-themed songs and songs that are special to the two of you.
- A dance mix
- A sad mix
- A sappy love song mix
- A personality mix: Dedicate the mix to someone you know (a friend, your dad, a sibling) and pick songs that remind you of that person and times you've spent together.

Decorate the cassette or CD case in the theme you've chosen.

WRITE IT! What would be the track list to *your* personality mix? In other words, what songs do you think capture your personality or moods? List at least 10–15 songs.

_____

_____

_____

_____

_____

_____

_____

_____

_____

_____

_____

_____

_____

_____

WORK IT! Get together with a friend or two and test how musically in sync you are. Take turns making up rhythms or melodies on the instrument of your choice — bang them out on your homemade rhythm maker, pick out notes on the piano, sing your own little song, or even stomp a rhythm on the floor. See if you can echo each other's rhythms or melodies exactly.

✳*WORK IT!* Try a little freestyling. Have a friend play a beat (on an instrument or just with his or her hands and feet) while you rap over it, making it up as you go along.

✳*WORK IT!* Do you already play an instrument or sing? Here are a few ideas you could try:

- Start your own band. Don't sweat it if you don't play guitar or drums — you'd be surprised how many different instruments can work in a rock band. (Sometimes I play violin in a band; the artists you hear on the radio use trumpet, flute, saxophone, cello, harmonica, and countless other instruments.) Or get a cheap guitar or bass and start practicing! Decide how many people you want in your band — usually three is the minimum — and whether you'll have one lead singer or take turns. Be sure to practice singing and playing at the same time — it's harder than it looks. You can start out by playing other people's songs, or "covering" them, if you want, but don't be afraid to dive in and write your own. You've got something to say!

- Take a shot at composing. Writing a song or a piece of music doesn't have to mean coming up with a huge, multilayered, multi-instrument work. Just you and your instrument, or even just your voice alone, is plenty to start with. You don't have to write it out — play around for a while with different note combinations and bits of melody and see what comes out. If you'd like to write a song, you can also try start-ing with the words — decide what you want to write about, then go from there.

- Try an improv jam session. Get together with a bunch of friends who also play or sing — at least two, but no more than five. Start out simple — come up with a basic beat or harmony, and take turns improvising melodies over that. Once you feel comfortable with that, try a looser approach: One person starts playing something, anything, and the others join in as inspiration strikes, weaving their own rhythms and melodies around what everyone else is doing. (This can be tricky at first, which is why I don't recommend doing it with more than five people to start with.)

Dance

Dance has been around for a long, long time — from rain dances to ballroom dances to school dances to the latest dance video, we use dance to connect with rhythm, and with one another. Music inspires us to move — it always has and probably always will. Dance adds a visual and physical element to music, connecting it even more deeply with the body. When you dance, or even just tap your feet to a tune, you're using your body to express the emotions that the music brings out.

You don't have to have master moves to enjoy

dance. The exercises here have nothing to do with the kind of dancing you do at a party, so don't worry if your footwork could use some work and your moves aren't so smooth.

☀"WORK IT!" WARMING UP: Pick out a piece of classical music on a CD or on the radio. Get into comfortable clothes, and move with the music. Don't worry about doing anything that looks like actual *dancing* — instead, just move your body around in a way that seems to fit the music. Do whatever feels right to you — swirl your arms around when the music sounds flowy and watery, jump up and down if the music has lots of strong beats, stand on your tiptoes and stretch up your arms as the music gets louder and louder, or anything else that you're inspired to do. Get your whole body involved — head, toes, hips, lips, every little bit of you.

☀"WORK IT!" Do the previous exercise, but this time do it with a pop or rock song. Do the kinds of movements you want to make feel different from the ones you did with the classical piece?

Not only can dance mimic what's going on in the music, it can also add another layer of meaning to music, acting out a story or expressing an idea. It can also act on its own without music — cheerleaders, for example, often do dance-inspired moves with no music at all.

☀"WORK IT!" Make up a dance routine to one of your favorite songs. Don't try to copy the video's choreography; instead, put the song on your CD player and listen to it a few times, paying attention to how the rhythms and melodies make you want to move. Does the music inspire quick, jerky movements or flowing, graceful gestures? You might feel like making up elaborate dance steps, or acting out the story of the song, or doing something more abstract. This can be a fun thing to do with friends. If you want, perform your masterpiece for friends or family when you're done.

☀"WORK IT!" Invent a rain dance. Don't feel like dancing for rain? Make up any kind of dance, as long as it expresses something that you really, really want — a good grade, a team victory, a new bike, a day at the beach. Find rhythms and movements that express or mimic what you're hoping for — swishy hand and body movements to imitate falling rain, for example, or clapping your hands and stamping your feet to make thunder sounds. Set it to music, have a friend drum out a beat, or just dance to silence.

Dance is highly physical by definition — you're moving your body. Without even trying, you can improve your coordination, your balance, and your fitness. You can also use it to explore what your body can do.

✴**"WORK IT!"** Practice an *arabesque,* the ballet term for when you stand on one leg with the other one extended out behind you. Start out just balancing on your left foot. When you've got that down, try lifting your right leg behind you, keeping it straight. How high can you lift it? As you bring it higher, you'll need to lean forward to balance yourself. Bend your left leg if

✂️***LINKS***
Turn to *Body and Mind,* **Chapter 3 (Working It), for more activities to explore your body's possibilities.**

you need to. (Warning: Don't lift it so far that it hurts! As soon as you feel a stretching in your legs, don't force yourself any farther.) Try it on the other side, too.

WORK IT! When I took ballet lessons (for a year, when I was six), we learned a technique to help keep from getting dizzy when you spin around and around. Frankly, I never really got the hang of it — I still got dizzy enough to puke. Maybe I did it wrong. Anyway, the idea, as I understood it, is: Focus your eyes on one particular point — a certain spot on the wall, a far-off tree. Keep focusing on that one point as you start to turn your body around — in other words, your head keeps facing forward as your body turns. When you can't keep your head facing forward anymore, whip it around really quickly and immediately focus on that one point again as your body keeps turning around. If you want to try it, start reeeeaaaallly slowly at first, and gradually speed up. Try not to fall down or puke.

✳ ***WORK IT!*** Dance until you drop. Well, not literally — just turn on some loud, fast music and dance around until you sweat!

Theater and film

Are you an actor? Theater and film can be great creative outlets even if you don't consider yourself the theatrical type. Onstage or on camera, we're free to explore other perspectives, other lives different from our own. By acting out a part, you get a chance to try on that character's life, in a safe way. You might not actually want to be a bank robber, or a vamp, or a soldier, but it's fun to inhabit their skin for a little while. Doing so can also introduce you to traits you have or secretly want to have — the free-spiritedness of the outlaw, the confidence of the vamp, or the bravery of the soldier could all be pieces of the whole you.

✔ ***REALITY CHECK*** Marianne loves exploring other sides of herself while doing plays and improv. "I like being onstage and having all eyes on me, because normally I'm a rather reserved person and don't attract a lot of attention. Drama is a great environment because the people are really accepting of each other and not judgmental."

✏️ "WRITE IT!" Make a list of 10 roles you'd love to play. These could be things you aspire to be in real life or total fantasies. (Some examples: a witch, an officer on a spaceship, a pioneer of the Old West, a war hero, a rock star, Babe Ruth, a member of royalty, a stockbroker, a belly dancer, a character from your favorite TV show.)

✳️ "WORK IT!" Spend an hour in one of the roles you just listed. Go about your routine (cleaning your room, watching TV, running errands), but imagine yourself in your new role. How would that person sit, stand, move, talk, interact with other people? How would your character react to, say, your dog making a mess in the kitchen? What does it feel like to be in that person's skin? Have friends or family members play other roles. Their characters don't have to fit with yours — it might be fun to see how a pioneer and a witch would interact! If you're too embarrassed to do this in front of other people, you can limit yourself to just hanging out at home, but it can be a silly adventure to see how the guy at the deli reacts to your princess-in-exile routine. Try doing it with a friend — that can help you feel less shy and make the whole thing more fun.

✳*WORK IT!* Find a speech from a play, book, movie, or TV show that you like or find interesting. Anything — a man tearfully confessing to a crime, an evil genius plotting her next crime, a bride's vows to her groom. Memorize the words and practice giving that speech to your mirror. Try on different emotions and styles of delivery. Overact and really throw yourself into it.

✳*WORK IT!* Choose a play or skit from a book to act out, or write your own. Cast your friends, make costumes, and build a set, as simple or as elaborate as you want.

✂ *LINKS*
Theater and film often incorporate the visual arts (in set design, costumes, camera angles, and lighting), as well as other performing arts. For more on exploring the visual arts, turn to Chapter 1 (Discover Your Inner Artist).

✹*WORK IT!* Film your own documentary. Using a video camera (if you don't have one, you can borrow or rent one), create a film account of a day in your life. Before you film, take special note of any images or faces you want to capture. With digital cameras, you can even easily edit your work and add cool effects on the computer.

✒*WRITE IT!* Write the screenplay for your own movie. If you need ideas, you can adapt a story you've already written, or write a cinematic version of the latest news headlines. Cast your friends and film it!

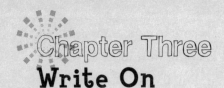

Chapter Three
Write On

The art of writing

> ✓ ***REALITY CHECK*** "I love to write," says Amy. "Being able to write is everything to me. I'm the editor of my school paper, and I write poetry and short stories. I know that I will write for the rest of my life, and if I weren't able to, the world would be a very sad and empty place."

Writing is a creative art that we use almost every day. We write to communicate, to share, and sometimes just to find our own voices. You probably write e-mail, notes, and letters to your friends, and you write things all the time in school. Maybe you keep a journal or a Web log, or you write stories or plays. Sometimes your writing can be as creative as you want, like in a letter, a story, or in your journal. Other times, you may feel like you can't be very creative at all in your writing — like when you write an assignment for a really strict teacher.

Writing has always been an important part of my

life, from the short stories I wrote in elementary school and the journals I started keeping in middle school to the articles and books that I'm lucky enough to get paid to write now. I've used it to share secrets, to escape from the real world, to work my way out of sadness, and to spread good news. And I truly believe that even if you don't consider yourself to be even a halfway decent writer, the act of putting words to paper can open you up to all the many parts of the whole you.

> "Writing and reading is to me synonymous with existing."
> — Gertrude Stein, author

For the exercises in this chapter (and for all the exercises in **The Whole You**), don't worry too much about spelling, punctuation, or grammar. While that stuff is very important in writing, right now it's much more important that you just get your ideas down.

WRITE IT! WARMING UP: Do two pages of *free writing.* To free write, sit down with pencil (or pen) and paper and just start writing. Write whatever comes into your head, and don't stop until you've done two pages. Keep going no matter what, even if all you write is something like "I don't know what to write about blah blah blah blah this is so stupid" over and over again. Seriously. It's good to do this by hand instead of on a computer, just to get the physical experience of putting your thoughts to paper.

Writing to communicate

One of the most basic uses of writing is to transmit information. When writing was first invented, it was used to keep track of supplies and spread news. We use it now not only for those purposes but to share emotions, express philosophical thoughts, and describe events. You write reports and essays in school to communicate facts and arguments, and you write letters or e-mail to communicate information, gossip, or feelings. Exploring different ways of communicating through the written word makes you better able not only to get your ideas and feelings across to others but to find the best way to show your whole self to the world.

> "Writing, when properly managed (as you may be sure I think mine is), is but a different name for conversation."
> — Laurence Sterne, novelist, *Tristram Shandy*

WRITE IT! Write about something that happened to you today. It can be big or small, happy or sad, silly or profound — anything that stuck in your mind. Pretend that you're explaining it to someone else. Include information like: Where were you? What happened? Was anyone else there? How did you feel about it? Do you feel differently now?

WRITE IT! Write a letter to a friend you haven't been in touch with for a long time. It could be a far-off camp friend, a cousin who lives across the country, even a friend from your school who you fought with once and haven't spoken to since. What do you wish you could tell him or her? If you want to, mail the letter.

WRITE IT! Every family has stories — the one about the time Jimmy tried to bring home a raccoon, the one about Great-grandma sneaking coded messages behind enemy lines, the one about how your parents met, the one about you as a baby. Write down a family story. Tell it in your words, the way you'd tell it if you were talking.

Just because you're communicating information doesn't mean that it has to be presented in a dry, straightforward way. A few typed paragraphs that answer who-what-when-where-why may work for a school report, but different approaches can be more fun to read *and* to write. Stretch your creative muscles by finding inventive new ways to convey the facts.

※ *"WORK IT!"* Create the front page of your very own newspaper. Make up a name for your paper, and write articles about what's going on in your life and the lives of your family, friends, and neighbors. What kinds of unique or unusual things can you include — a survey about your family members' favorite dinners? An investigative report of the neighbor kid's dating habits? A local weather forecast? If you feel really ambitious, you could lay it out using a computer program like PageMaker, but that's not necessary — just write or type each article, and lay them out in a newspaper format using glue and tape. Photocopy the pages for a professional look and hand them out to family members, or send them to far-off friends and relatives as an update on what's going on in your world.

WRITE IT! Write a poem about an important event in your life. Don't worry about making it rhyme — make it as free-form as you want.

WRITE IT! In his play *Rosencrantz and Guildenstern Are Dead,* Tom Stoppard imagined what Shakespeare's *Hamlet* would be like rewritten from the point of view of two minor characters. Write about an event that happened to you or someone you know, but do it from the point of view of someone not directly related to the action. So, for example, if you and your friend got into a fight at a convenience store, you could write about it from the point of view of the store's cashier.

Think in ink

Writing can be a very powerful way to express your thoughts and feelings, not only to other people but to yourself. It can help you figure out exactly what you're feeling when your mind's a mess, and it can help you get your thoughts in order. Writing can also help you understand yourself better, relieve stress, and remind you of what's important to you. And it gives you someone to talk to (yourself!) when you've got something that is so important — or so random — you don't feel like telling anyone else.

✂*LINKS*
See *Spirit*, Chapter 1 ("Who Am I?"), for more WRITE IT! exercises to help you discover the whole you.

✏*WRITE IT!* Ever get in an argument with someone (your friend, your mom, an unfair teacher) who just won't listen to your side of the story? Write out what you wish you could have told the person. Explain exactly what happened or what you think. Don't hold back — this is for your eyes only.

"If writing did not exist, what terrible depressions we should suffer from."
— Sei Shonagon, diarist and writer

✏*WRITE IT!* Write about something good that happened today. It could be huge (you won an award) or small (they had your favorite meal in

✂*LINKS*
Turn to *Spirit*, Chapter 6 (Peace Out!), for more on finding the good in each day.

the cafeteria, your shirt smelled great straight out of the laundry). Why was it so great? How exactly did it make you feel? After it happened, did you feel differently about the day?

➤ "WRITE IT!" Write through a decision you're trying to make — again, it can be big or small. (Should you go out for the basketball team? Can you really trust this friend with your secret? What's the best way to ask your mom for some cash?) But write it as if you're two different people arguing each side of the decision. So, for example, if I were trying to decide whether or not I wanted to go to a certain party, I could start writing the argument like this:

PRO: Well, if you go to the party, you could have a lot of fun. You like going to parties, right?

CON: But you won't know anyone at this party! What if you end up standing in the corner all night, not talking to anyone?

PRO: But maybe you'll meet some really

cool people! Weren't you just saying the other day that you wanted to make some new friends?

Write through it until you reach some kind of conclusion or decision.

Journals are another way that we use writing to find ourselves. They not only help you work things through, they help you know yourself better, keep perspective on your whole self, even keep your creativity flowing. Most important, they can be a major tool you can use in the exploration that you've started with **The Whole You.** By keeping a journal, you learn a little bit about yourself every day that you write, and by looking back at your journal, you remind yourself of who you are, or who you once were.

✳ *"WORK IT!"* A journal doesn't have to be just a straight retelling of what happened to you each day; it can be a creative project in its own right. Here are some different kinds of journals you can try:

A quote journal: Collect quotes and poems that are meaningful to you. You can just write them down, or if you like, note the date you added each quote to your journal, and include a few lines about why you chose to keep that quote or how it expresses what you're going through.

A free-writing journal: Whenever you write, do it as quickly as you can without stopping, jotting down anything that comes into your head — and I mean *anything*, no matter how random it seems.

A collage journal: Use fragments of pictures, words, and articles cut from magazines and newspapers to create collages that fit your current mood.

✂ *LINKS*
Turn to Chapter 1 (Discover Your Inner Artist) for more ways to express what's inside you using images and colors.

A color journal: Pick different colors to write in according to your moods.

A scrapbook journal: Combine the classic scrapbook with the classic journal — paste photos, ticket stubs, and other memorabilia in your journal, and write about why they're important to you.

A letter journal: This journal is something

you share with a close friend. First you write a letter to your friend, then give her or him the journal. Then your friend writes one to you and gives the journal back. Keep trading the journal back and forth until it's full.

A dream journal: Keep track of the wild world of your subconscious by writing about your nighttime dreams. Place this journal by your bedside, so you can jot down all your dreams as soon as you wake up, when they're freshest in your mind.

A thanksgiving journal: This journal has nothing to do with the turkey holiday. Each day, write down at least one thing that you are thankful for that day. This reminds you that no matter how

> *LINKS*
> **Read more about the benefits of thankfulness in** *Spirit,* **Chapter 6 (Peace Out!).**

crummy the day, there's always something good in it.

A poetry journal: Write musings on life, your moods, your dreams — all in poetry. Some days you might feel like rhyming, some days you might feel like being crazily free-form; some days you might feel like writing almost like you're talking, some days you might just describe a series of random images. Sticking to a poetry-only rule might seem hard, but it can actually free you up to try funky new things with your writing.

A video or audio journal: (Yeah, I know — technically this isn't writing. I'm okay with that if you are.) Set up a video camera or Web cam and pretend you're in the *Real World* confessional. Or carry a mini recorder around with you everywhere, so you can rattle off random thoughts whenever they strike. You'll have your very own documentary of life as you know it. (Now you just have to figure out what to do with 3,000 hours' worth of video. . . .)

Of course, feel free to combine elements of any or all of these journal types, or invent your own! It's also important to pick a book or notebook for your journal that you love writing in, whether it's one of those fancy diaries with a lock and key or just a plain spiral notebook. I've always kept my journal in a clothbound book with unlined paper, the kind with a ribbon bookmark sewn in, because I love the old-fashioned feeling. My friend Megan can write only in those retro black-and-white composition notebooks. Most bookstores and office-supply stores have a wide range of journals and notebooks to choose from. Pick whatever works best for you, and don't forget to decorate your journal's cover and pages, if that's what you like. Maybe your medium of choice is your computer — type your musings into a locked file, or post them on the Internet in a Web log.

Creative cartwheels

Writing is my favorite way to be creative. I do it pretty much every day. But even professional writers need a creativity boost once in a while. Here are some exercises that I use to get my creative juices flowing:

> **WRITE IT!** Pick an everyday object in the room you're sitting in — a cup, a pencil, a bookshelf, a shoe. Describe it for someone who has never seen one before and has no idea what it's for.

> **WRITE IT!** Pick another object in the room you're in. Describe it, inventing a pretend history

for it. For example, you could pick an ordinary No. 2 pencil and say: "This pencil has been handed down in my family from generation to generation since the Civil War. My great-great-grandfather used this pencil to write a letter to my great-great-grandmother, asking her to marry him. . . ."

WRITE IT! Think of a person you know. What food item does he or she remind you of? (A cherry Popsicle? A grimy potato? A root beer float? A Thanksgiving turkey? A strip of beef jerky?) Write one paragraph comparing that person to the food.

WRITE IT! Start with the words "I don't know" and keep going wherever your pen takes you.

WRITE IT! Describe a room in your house in as much detail as you can. Here's the catch: Don't go into that room or look at it. Describe it totally from memory. When you're done, compare your description to the real-life room. What kinds of things did you remember, and what kinds of things did you forget?

WRITE IT! Write a story starting with any of these sentences:

- **It was the worst day of Bobby Parker's life.**
- **Miranda didn't believe in ghosts.**
- **When the Chen family looked back on that day, they often wondered what went wrong.**
- **Once upon a time, there was a very little girl with a very big nose.**
- **"I can't believe you did this to me," Janey sobbed.**
- **Grandpa loved to tell us the story of how our family came to settle in Alaska.**
- **There were a few things Chris knew for sure.**
- **It all started when Tara found the magic beans.**

65

Feel free to change the names to ones of your own invention. Your story can be funny, sad, serious, happy, short, long, simple, complicated, anything you like. For a real challenge, use the same sentence to start a funny story *and* a sad story. If you want more prompts, you can look for starting points in the world around you. Have a friend make up a first sentence for you, then you do the same for your friend. Use random sentences you overhear strangers saying — wandering around the mall and hanging out at a coffee shop are two great ways to collect bits of people's lives. Or find a headline in the newspaper ("Man Rescues Boy from Shark Attack," "Homeless Grandmother Celebrates 101st Birthday") and use it to inspire your own version of what might have happened.

WORK IT! Pick your favorite fairy tale or adventure story, and rewrite it in the voice of the villain or an unsympathetic character. (Think Cinderella from the mean stepmother's perspective, or *Harry Potter and the Sorcerer's*

Stone from the point of view of Snape or Malfoy.)

Writing with a different brain

Most of us have a preferred method of writing. Some people like to write on a computer; others like to write with a pen or a pencil. Some people prefer certain kinds of paper or pens. Such a method makes you feel comfortable and secure.

But sometimes interesting creative inspiration hits when you're *not* comfortable, when you shake things up a little. One way to shake up the writing process is to try using different tools to write. Using different tools actually makes you *think* differently, and thus write differently. For example, writing on a computer, where you can instantly change your mind about words and phrases and delete your mistakes, means that you write very differently from when you write with a pen on paper, where you can't change anything without crossing it out, and you feel the words flowing from your hand right onto the page. Or if you're not a very good typist, writing on a computer might slow you down. Doing something differently works different parts of your brain and shows you different parts of yourself.

"WRITE IT!" Pick any writing exercise from this chapter. Do this exercise using tools you wouldn't ordinarily choose. Here are some different tools you can try:

- If you like to write on a computer, write by hand. If you usually write by hand, try writing on a computer.
- Try different writing utensils: pen, pencil, crayon, marker, paintbrush, chalk, fountain pen, lipstick, finger paint.
- Use different colors. Does it feel different to write in purple, blue, red, green, pink highlighter, silver marker? You can also try writing in different colors on your computer.
- On a computer, try different fonts. Pick your favorite fonts, but also try writing in a font you think is really ugly.
- Use your nondominant hand. (If you're right-handed, use your left, and if you're left-handed, use your right.)

Giving yourself mental challenges while you write can sometimes inspire creative solutions, too.

✎•WRITE IT!• Try to write a few sentences without a single word that contains the letter "e." Could you write a whole story like that?

✳•WORK IT!• Take a few sheets of newspaper and cut out random words from headlines and ads. Rearrange the words into a poem, as silly or as serious as you like. Use *only* the words available.

✂•LINKS•
The book *A Void,* by Georges Perec, is a novel written entirely without the letter "e." It was originally written in French (in French, it's titled *La Disparation*), then translated into English — and *neither* version contains a single "e." Whew!

✂•LINKS•
Turn to Appendix A (Books to Indulge Your Creativity) for more sources of written inspiration.

69

Chapter Four
Create Something!

Get creative with creativity

> ✔ ***REALITY CHECK*** Chelsye is into all kinds of creative activities — not just playing music, acting in plays, drawing, and writing. "I write comic books, one with a few friends and one by myself. I love to cook — I come up with some of the weirdest things in the kitchen, but they all taste good. I decorate my backpack with buttons and pins, and my locker with pictures of friends, newspaper clippings, and photos. I have been known to throw some great parties, and usually I win my own costume contests."

Up till now, we've been exploring all the traditional "artistic" ways to be creative. But there are millions of other ways to express creativity — basically, to create things — besides the typical arts. Even if you're not into the classic kinds of artistic expression that we talked about in Chapters 1 to 3, you might like other kinds of creation. Through the process of making something or expressing yourself in a creative way, you always learn something, whether it's about the craft or about yourself, and that gets added to the picture of the whole you. There's also the satisfaction you get from creating something of your own.

✔ *REALITY CHECK* "I love the experience of creating something that has my name or style written all over it — that someone will see it and say, 'That's really neat,'" says Chelsye. "I also enjoy the time you spend on yourself, because you're creating from inside you. No one can take that away from you."

Some other areas where you can wield your creative energies are:

Crafts. These can include sewing, knitting, woodworking, furniture building, candle making, sand castle creating, friendship bracelet making, sticker collecting, origami, face painting, balloon animal making, and more.

✳ **"WORK IT!"** Feeling crafty? Here are 21 easy activities to inspire you (ask a parent if you need help with any of these):

1. Learn to knit.
2. Invent the world's greatest paper airplane.
3. Throw a theme party. First, think of a theme — pirates? Harry Potter? 1970s glam? Next, come up with ways you can use the theme in your decorations and snacks. For a glam theme, you could decorate your house or party space to look like a disco, with blinking lights and a mirror ball. Serve retro foods like cheese fondue and Charleston Chews, and play groovy 1970s music. For a Harry Potter theme, you could model your living room after the Hogwarts Great Hall, the Gryffindor common room, or maybe Snape's dungeon. Invent your own versions of the magical foods in the books.

Make invitations that go with your theme, and encourage guests to dress up!

4. Make sock puppets. Decorate with scraps of fabric and odds and ends from around the house (buttons, ribbon, Styrofoam pellets, whatever you can find).

5. Make a scrapbook. Buy a photo album or premade scrapbook from a bookstore or craft store, or make your own by stapling, tying, or somehow binding together sheets of heavy paper. (Get creative with how you bind the paper together!) Glue bits of memorabilia (ticket stubs, an envelope filled with dried flower petals, photos, letters, cards) onto the pages. You can buy specially made photo corners to help stick things down, if you don't want to glue them directly. Be sure to write captions explaining what everything is. Decorate the cover.

> *LINKS*
> Check out Chapter 3 (Write On) for more scrapbook and journal ideas.

6. Make a 100-foot-long paper chain. (You remember how to do it: Bend a strip of

paper into a loop, and tape it closed. Slip another strip through the middle, bend it into a loop, and tape it closed. And so on.) Use any kind of paper you want — newspaper, construction paper, printer paper, whatever. When you're done, figure out what the heck you'll do with 100 feet of paper chain: Hang it all over your room? Decorate the Christmas tree? Adorn the front porch?

7. Get some body paint, or borrow different colors of makeup from someone who wears it, and turn your legs into your personal canvas.

8. Make flowers out of tissue paper.

9. Make papier-mâché monsters.

10. Plant something — a tulip bulb, a potato piece, an ivy plant. Take care of it and watch it grow.

11. Build a kite.

12. Make paper snowflakes.

13. Decorate a (clean and empty) jelly jar or frozen juice can to make a pencil holder.

14. Construct a fort.

15. Make your own holiday cards.

16. Find a brick or a largish rock. Paint and decorate it, and use it as a doorstop or paperweight.

17. Make masks out of paper plates, paper bags, cardboard cut into shapes, anything you can think of. Be sure to decorate them.

18. Tie daisy stems together to make a chain.

19. Collect scraps of wood from the park, woods, or beach. Construct a boat, a bookshelf, a weird sculpture — whatever you're inspired to do.

20. Tie-dye a T-shirt, pillowcase, or other fabric piece.

21. Make a glitter globe. Put glitter, sequins, metallic confetti, and anything else you like in a clear glass jar. Fill the jar up to the very top with cold water, and screw on the lid as tight as you can. You might want to seal the top with glue to make sure it doesn't leak. Experiment with different amounts of glittery stuff. You

can also glue figures or little scenes to the inside of the jar lid, and watch them sit through the glitter storm!

Cooking. Not just cooking, but baking, grilling, lemonade making, sandwich construct-ing, cake decorating, and all kinds of food fancies. Cooking is a wonderful way to be creative because your creations nourish you and others. Food tastes great when you make it yourself. And think how fun and satisfying it is to be able to feed your friends or family! Here are some basic food experiments you can try:

✂○*LINKS*
For more on food and how it fuels you, grab *Body and Mind* and flip to Chapter 2 (Eat Up!).

✳*WORK IT!* Invent your own fruit punch. Mix together different juices (apple, orange, grape, cranberry, whatever you like) to make your own tasty combination. Add ginger ale or another kind of soda if you like. (My personal favorite is orange juice, cranberry juice, and a little seltzer, all mixed together.) When you hit on something you like, be sure to write down what you put in it so you can re-create your masterpiece. (If this doesn't sound too thrilling to you, go for the opposite goal: the most disgusting concoction you can come up with!)

WORK IT! Try cooking something from a recipe. Grab a cookbook and pick out something that sounds tasty to you. Read the instructions carefully, and ask for help (and permission!) from an adult before going crazy with the stove or lots of knives.

WORK IT! Feed your friends! Next time you have a bunch of friends over, instead of popping open a pint of ice cream or a bag of chips, find things you can cook or make for them. Stuff you can make together is fun, too. Premade cookie dough is one easy place to start, but if you feel more ambitious, try these:

- Make your own guacamole or cheese dip for chips and veggies.
- Bake a cake or cupcakes that you can decorate together.

77

- Make pigs-in-blankets — hot dogs rolled up in that prefab croissant dough and baked.
- Go for homemade fries — cut up potatoes, toss with olive oil, salt, and pepper, spread on a cookie sheet, and bake at 400 degrees Fahrenheit for a half hour or so, or until crispy (turn the pieces over once or twice while they're baking).
- Make mini pizzas with an English muffin or mini-bagel halves, tomato sauce, and shredded cheese. Broil in a toaster oven or microwave 'em until the cheese melts. Again, ask an adult for help if you're not used to using the stove or oven.

WORK IT! If you're already accomplished in the kitchen — like, most of the activities in this section seem way too easy for you — throw a dinner party! Invite four or five friends over for dinner, and sit down with whichever of your parents is a better cook to plan the menu.

Remember, *you're* going to cook most of this, not your mom or dad, but they can help you figure out what to serve and assist with shopping and table setting.

Fashion. Every time you decide what outfit to put on in the morning, you're making a creative decision — especially when you do something a little different to personalize your threads. Ever feel like making your own clothes? Or wearing a kooky hat, doodling on your backpack, trying out funky earrings or a new 'do? That's all creative. Here are some fashion-forward things to try:

✳ **"WORK IT!"** Grab a plain T-shirt, any color. Decorate it using permanent markers or fabric paint. (Be sure to put cardboard or something inside the shirt while you're working so the ink or paint doesn't bleed through.) Or sew or glue on sequins, beads, rhinestones, ribbon trim, or other decorations. Stitch your initials on, or paint it in your school colors. Use your computer to make an iron-on of your favorite photo. Think creatively — want to cut off the sleeves or shred them into fringe 1980s style? Want to slice the crewneck into a V-neck and lace it up with ribbon? Go for it!

✳ *"WORK IT!"* Paint your nails in cool designs. (Guys, you can do this, too!) Make each toenail a different color.

✳ *"WORK IT!"* Go through a bunch of magazines and cut out pictures of people (celebrities, models, politicians, anyone) you think look cool. Try to pick photos that are all about the same size. Cut each picture up into head, torso, and legs, and use the pieces to mix and match different combos of hair, tops, and pants/skirts. Throw guys and girls together, just to mix it up a little more. Use the outfits for inspiration for your own funky outfits. Tuxedo jacket and peasant skirt? Camouflage and skater shoes? Dreadlocks and satin? There's no limit to what you can dream up!

*"WORK IT!" Make the most fabulous Halloween costume ever. Instead of buying something prefab from the store, create it yourself. Dye your hair, paint your face, buy or make the perfect clothes, construct your own props.

*"WORK IT!" Funkify your backpack. You've got to wear it every day, so it might as well scream YOU. Use permanent (waterproof) markers to doodle on designs, cover it with buttons and pins, stitch on cool patches or iron-ons, tie ribbons on every inch of it, dye it different colors, whatever expresses you best. (Be sure to check with your parents before doing anything permanent!)

> ***LINKS***
> See Chapter 1 (Discover Your Inner Artist) for more on turning everyday objects into fantastic works of art.

*"WORK IT!" Bored with that belt? Think of other things you can use to hold up your pants. The only requirement is that whatever you use be long and thin. Think: a rope, a ribbon, a telephone cord, a super-long licorice string (not recommended in hot or wet weather!), a braid of twine or yarn, a scarf, a strip of cool fabric, a chain, a beaded cord.

You probably haven't ventured into every single kind of creativity before, so take the opportunity to try something new. When you stretch yourself creatively, you build up brainpower in new areas, and you discover new things about yourself, whether it's a love of poetry or an insight into how to meet new challenges. Opening your mind to new creative possibilities develops not just your artistic side, but the whole you, too.

WORK IT! For one whole week, try one new creative activity a day. The key is that it has to be really *new* — so if you have a favorite way to be creative, try something completely different, preferably something you never do. If you write, bake a cake; if you paint, pick up a kazoo — anything to get you using different creative muscles. Use the activities in this chapter and Chapters 1 to 3 for inspiration.

LINKS
Check out the books listed in Appendix A (Books to Indulge Your Creativity) for more activities to try.

82

Combining the arts

You've probably noticed that a lot of the "other" cre-ativities that we've talked about so far have elements of the classic arts in them — fashion, furniture build-ing, and cake decorating, for example, all deal with the visual arts in some way. This mixing of the arts not only stimulates more parts of the whole you, it engages your brain in new and cool ways. You can combine the arts with one another and with other activities for a more complex creative experience — one that appeals to more parts of the whole you.

Here are some combinations you might want to try:

WORK IT! *Visual arts and writing:*

- Make a poem poster. On a sheet of poster board, write poems and quotes you love in different colors, shapes, and sizes. Illus-trate them if you like, and add other dec-orations. Fill every inch of the board.
- Create a word picture. Pick a long poem or piece of text — like a passage from your favorite book, or, ideally, something you wrote yourself. Think of an image

that goes with your text — for example, you might pick the image of a bird in flight to go with a description of your soul soaring. On a piece of paper, lightly outline your image in pencil. Write your chosen text inside this outline so it "colors in" the image. If you want, you can write in a variety of colors to give the drawing colored details, or just use different thicknesses of letters to create details — like making one or two heavier letters right where the bird's eye would be.

- Write a story and design a cover for it.
- Make your own 'zine or Web 'zine.
- Create a comic book.

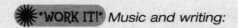

WORK IT! *Music and writing:*

- Write your own song, lyrics and all.
- Write rap lyrics to go over a classical music piece you like.
- Write a story to go with a piece of music. It could be the story you think the music

is telling, a story inspired by the feeling of the music, or a story that has the music as part of the plot.

※*"WORK IT!" *Visual arts and music:*

- While listening to any kind of music, create an image that seems to express what's in the music. Paint it, sculpt it, draw it, collage it, whatever seems fitting to you.
- Some people naturally "see" colors that go with certain notes and chords. Try thinking about color and sound yourself. Listen to any kind of music. What kinds of colors go with it in your head? (It may help to think about what *emotions* the music evokes for you, then think about what colors go with those emotions.)

※*"WORK IT!" *Film and music and dance:*

- Film your own music video, set to the song of your choice.

✳***WORK IT!*** *Theater and music:*

- Take in a musical or an opera.
- Act out your own silent film, set to whatever kind of music you like.

✳***WORK IT!*** *Theater and visual arts and crafts:*

- Design and build the set and props for your own play or film.

✳***WORK IT!*** *Theater and writing and music:*

- Write a short play, and think of pop songs that could fit in as part of the story line.

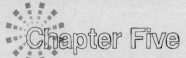

Curiosity Counts

Why curiosity counts

Curiosity and creativity are deeply intertwined. That's because in order to be creative, it's important to be open to and curious about the world as well as yourself. Curiosity helps introduce you to new ideas, new ways of thinking, even new parts of yourself that you never knew existed — which, by the way, is the whole point of **The Whole You**. All of these new things get swirled around and added to your unique creative mix.

Many great creations started with someone's curiosity, someone saying "I wonder . . . ?" or "What if . . . ?" Curiosity motivates and inspires you to follow your flights of fancy. It aids experimentation and fuels imagination. By following your curiosity wherever it may lead, you might just find yourself with a new creation, new knowledge, even a new hobby.

> "I think, at a child's birth, if a mother could ask a fairy god-mother to endow it with the most useful gift, that gift would be curiosity."
> — Eleanor Roosevelt, U.S. First Lady, author, speaker, activist, diplomat

✔ ***REALITY CHECK*** "I join lots of activities just because I'm curious to find out more about them," says Marianne. "In sixth grade, I heard about some kid who played the oboe. I played the clarinet, and I was getting bored with it. At my school I dug up a really decrepit oboe from a storage room and just started experimenting with it. My clarinet teacher was furious and told me, 'You're such a good clarinet player! Stick with it!' But I really wanted to try a new instrument. I taught myself the basics of the oboe, then I finally started oboe lessons. I've loved it ever since, and this year I quit clarinet for good."

Chelsye found her love of comic books by following her curiosity. "My friend Jon got me hooked on comic books in seventh grade," she says. "Then he and another friend started working on the comic book they make. Eventually, they asked me if I would like to help write it!"

➡ ***WRITE IT!*** List 10 subjects you wish you knew more about (surfing, astronomy, World

War II, architecture, your new favorite TV
star . . .).

_____

_____

_____

_____

_____

_____

_____

_____

_____

Where do you think you could find out
more about them — search the Internet? Go to the library? Talk to someone who does the activity? Write down
as many ideas as you can for each
subject. Do one of those things today.

> **✂ *LINKS***
> **Flip to Appendix
> B (Research
> Resources) for
> more ideas on
> where to go to
> find out what
> you need to
> know.**

✳ *WORK IT!* This week, your assignment is to
learn about one thing that you've never heard
about before. First, I know what you're think-

ing — how do you find the thing you're going to learn about if you've never heard of it before? Start by grabbing a newspaper, or ask your mom or dad for one of their magazines. Flip through, skimming over the headlines and articles until something catches your eye that you don't know anything about. It doesn't have to be the president of some obscure country — maybe it's a band whose show is reviewed in the arts section or a sports figure who's new to you. A foreign film, a new law passed by Congress, a holiday you don't know about, even something from a department store ad (what the heck is "cloisonné"?) could spark your interest. If newspapers and magazines don't inspire you, try flipping through an encyclopedia or atlas, or even picking a random ingredient from a food package label (lecithin, anyone?).

Once you've figured out what your research victim is, it's time to dive in. Start by reading whatever article or ad you found it in. Then get creative about how you can learn more. Check out the library. Or maybe that band has a Web site or that new law you're curious about is featured on a news Web site for kids. (Again, Appendix B has some places you can look.) You can look up some things in a dictionary ("cloisonné" comes to mind) or encyclopedia. Ask sports-obsessed friends if they've heard of the person you're interested in, or find the team Web site. Call the food company's toll-free number and ask what in the world lecithin is.

Now, I don't want you to think that curiosity is important only when it relates to some big, meaty subject. Curiosity can lead to creativity and inspiration even when the subject of your curiosity isn't that weighty — no, *especially* when it's not that weighty. In fact, curiosity about the little things in life can often result in the most surprising discoveries.

✳ *WORK IT!* For one day, write down every single question that comes into your head, no matter how random or stupid it seems to you. (Why are letters arranged the way they are on a computer keyboard? Where does toe jam come from? Is my sister an alien? Why doesn't my teacher ever assign interesting books?)

This is kind of a more grown-up version of being five years old and asking "why?" every two minutes!

Now spend the next day finding answers to at least half of those questions. Some you can look up in the library or on the Internet (see Appendix B for those research resources again). For others, you might have to ask parents or teachers, though I recommend *not* asking your teacher why he or she never assigns interesting books! Write all your questions and answers out in a notebook to create your own Book of Questions.

If you do the question-asking exercise above, you'll probably find yourself with a lot of weird trivia on your hands. That's a good thing! Curious people absorb random bits of knowledge — how to tie a fisherman's knot, the circumference of the Earth — because they take an interest in many different corners of the world. Adding to your store of supposedly useless knowledge keeps your brain and imagination fired up and adds dimension to the whole you. And frankly, it's also fun!

☀ "WORK IT!" This week, acquire one fun new skill or piece of knowledge. Here are some ideas:

- Teach yourself how to say a random sentence in a new language. For inspiration, hit the travel section of your local bookstore. Many travel guides have phrase book sections in them; you can also find phrase books published just for travelers. These are chock-full of fun phrases like "This meat is underdone" and "Where is the embassy?" Be sure to pick a language not offered at your school (Hungarian, Swahili, Danish) and then mystify all around you when you toss off *yuketsu o shinaide kudasai* ("I don't want a blood transfusion" in Japanese).
- Learn how to whistle.
- Memorize all the lyrics to a new song.
- Pick up a magic trick.
- Learn how to skate or blade backward.
- Perfect your swan dive.

- Learn how to walk on your hands.
- Any birds with distinctive calls or songs hanging out in your area? Practice imitating one until you get it perfect.

Open up

Open-mindedness is another crucial component of both curiosity and creativity. Being open-minded means being open to new and different things, including new and possibly wacky ideas of your own. It's very difficult to grow and be whole if you're not open to new ideas and experiences and to learning about yourself. And without open-mindedness, it's practically impossible to be creative, since creativity requires new and different thinking.

Luckily, open-mindedness, like curiosity in general, occurs naturally in younger people. And even if you haven't had a chance to exercise your natural open-mindedness very much, it's a lot easier to develop it now than when you get older and more set in your ways.

WRITE IT! Quiz: Rate your open-mindedness

Is your mind wide open, or closed for business? Take this quiz and find out.

1. At your cousin's wedding, you're served something for dinner you've never seen before. All you know is it's weird and squirmy-looking and covered in some kind of sauce. Do you try it?
   a. You might nibble on it, but you're not going to dive in until you know exactly what it is.
   b. Sure — you love trying mystery meat.
   c. No way! And what kind of weirdo makes people eat this stuff, anyway?
2. Your dad sits you down and forces you to watch a nature special on TV — he says you need to branch out a little. Your most likely reaction?
   a. You sulk through the whole thing. Why do parents like the most boring things?
   b. After you get over missing your favorite show, you actually get into it a little. (But just a *little,* Dad — let's not make this a regular thing.)

95

   c. No one has to force you to watch any-
      thing — you love surfing around and find-
      ing weird new programs.

3. The new kid in school dresses like a refugee
from the 1970s — polyester bell-bottoms, plat-
form disco boots, beaded headbands, zip-
pered jumpsuits. (If for some reason these
clothes are considered *très* cool at your
school, substitute whatever would stand out
as wacky and out of touch.) What do you
think?

   a. You're totally into it — you love when
      people make a crazy fashion statement.

   b. Ugh, what a freak.

   c. Whatever — you don't really pay much
      attention.

4. Do you have any friends who are radically different from you?

   a. Maybe one or two — you're mainly drawn
      to people who are a lot like you, though.

   b. No. The whole point of friendship is hav-
      ing things in common, isn't it?

   c. Lots — you like mixing with different kinds
      of people. Even if you don't always under-

stand each other, they can teach you plenty.

10–12 points: Your mind is just about as open as they come. You're into trying new things, accepting new ideas, and you're always enthusiastic about people who dare to be different. All those new ideas careening into your brain are bound to keep your creativity humming!

Scoring:
1. a=2, b=3, c=1
2. a=1, b=2, c=3
3. a=3, b=1, c=2
4. a=2, b=1, c=3

7–9 points: Though you're willing to try new stuff sometimes, other times you'd rather not bother. Don't be afraid to take the plunge more often — you don't have to go crazy, but the more new stuff you're open to experiencing, the more exciting your life can get.

4–6 points: You seem to be a little uncomfortable with "weird" new experiences. Maybe that's because you're happy with your life the way it is. That's fine, but try to open up just a little bit. When you close yourself off to all that "weird" stuff, you miss out on a lot that could end up being really fun.

Swerve a little

We've already seen how entertaining and interesting random knowledge can be. I think it's important to invite randomness into *all* parts of your life. Often the most surprising and unexpected things that happen in life can be the most meaningful. Swerving from the straight-and-narrow, perfectly planned path once in a while and following your curiosity down a random road can lead to fun, creative experiences.

✄ ***LINKS***
To read more about finding new and exciting adventures, flip to Chapter 6 (The Adventure of Being You). For more on being open to yourself and everyone around you, turn to *Spirit,* Chapter 5 (Accepting Yourself — and Everyone Else).

My freshman year of college I was a very good student — I was paranoid that I wouldn't measure up to all the brilliant people around me, so I spent hours every day studying and doing schoolwork. I'm proud of the good grades I got, but my fondest memories of that school year are not of studying or getting my grades back. In particular, I remember one night during winter exams when I left my desk and ran outside to teach a friend how to make snow angels. (He was from California and had never seen snow before!) That silly experience — and great memory —

was possible only because I was willing to take a break from the strict program I set myself.

Now, just so your parents don't get mad at me, I'm not saying you should immediately blow off homework and go make snow angels. But when life presents you with an unexpected opportunity, no matter how small, don't assume you have to automatically turn it down just because it doesn't fit in with the plan. Be open to life's craziness!

Chapter Six
The Adventure of Being You

Live adventurously!

"Adventure?" you're asking. "What the heck does adventure have to do with being creative?" Stick with me for a second here.

To live creatively, I think it's important to have a personal sense of adventure. This doesn't necessarily mean you should be going on a safari next week, although of course that is a type of adventure. Having a sense of adventure simply means being willing to expand your horizons, explore possibilities, and venture into the unknown and exciting. Creativity itself is an adventure, since by definition every time you do something creative or tap into your creative self you're doing something new, different, and exciting.

> "Life is either a daring adventure, or nothing."
> — Helen Keller, author and lecturer

What do I mean by an adventure? Physical challenges count, like hiking a difficult trail, but challenging yourself emotionally or mentally counts as an adventure, too. Whether it's physical or mental, adventure introduces you to your inner strength. When you dive into an adventure or meet a challenge, you get to see new levels of complexity in your own character. You'll understand yourself more completely and feel a more powerful sense of your whole self.

✓ **"REALITY CHECK"** Heather found adventure when she went away to camp. "I met new friends there who basically became like my sisters," she remembers. "It gave me time to get away and just take care of myself and have fun."

Chelsye found a different kind of adventure when she had a chance to travel to South Africa. "The plane ride was twenty-four hours — that alone was enough to be considered an adventure!"

➤ **"WRITE IT!"** Fantasize about your ultimate adventure. Where would you go? What would you do? Write it all down, in lots of detail.

Adventure is totally wrapped up with open-mindedness and curiosity and all that good stuff. To live adventurously, you've got to be open to change and new experiences.

Breaking out of your routine and looking for new-ness is a key way to find adventure. It takes creativity to add mini-adventures to your daily life — one way to make sure you never get bored.

✂️ ***LINKS***
Flip back to Chapter 5 (Curiosity Counts) for more on how opening up can bring fresh adventure and creative inspiration.

🌟***WORK IT!*** Break out of your regu-lar routine. Every day for a week, do one thing that's totally out of charac-ter. Go for a jog instead of watching TV, get your chicken wings extra-spicy — it doesn't have to be earth-shattering, just different. How do these changes make you feel?

By finding adventure in everyday life, you add a lit-tle creativity to the whole you each day. It's fun to seek out bigger adventures, too. Even if you can't actually go on a safari, there are ways to add excitement on a smaller scale.

🌟***WORK IT!*** What was your ultimate fantasy adventure (in the exercise on page 101)? Is there a way that you can do even a tiny part of your adventure now? If your adventure is to sail around the world, can you take a sailing lesson? If your adventure is to climb Mount Everest, can you try rock climbing or hiking? If you'd like to explore the wildlife of the rain forest, can you volunteer at the zoo? If you dream of being a rock star, can you pick up a guitar, bust out at karaoke night, or get a rock-star haircut?

WORK IT! Play explorer: Ask one of your parents to take you to a nearby town or park where you've never been. With your parent, but without using a map, explore the area. Wander wherever your curiosity takes you.

WORK IT! 16 Creative Adventures to Have Before You Turn 16

1. Get together with friends to make a movie or TV show about your lives.
2. Express yourself with a (fake) tattoo or other body art.

✂ *LINKS*
Body and Mind,
**Chapter 2 (Eat
Up!), contains
tons of ways
to rev up your
palate.**

3. Try an unusual food you've never eaten before. Bonus points if you try something that really grosses you out and you end up liking it. Some suggestions: sushi, caviar, kidneys, escargots, tripe, seaweed, beet juice.

4. Learn to play a musical instrument — badly is okay.

5. At least once, make all of your holiday gifts yourself.

6. Wear something that's completely different from what you usually wear. If you're preppy, go punk, or vice versa.

7. Lose yourself: Get so caught up in your writing (or drawing, or dancing, or songwriting, or whatever) that you stay up all night.

8. Create a heartfelt poem, song, or painting for your crush. (You don't have to actually show it to anyone.)

9. Sing in public.

10. Make something that you can wear — a shirt, a pair of earrings, tie-dyed

shoelaces, a Halloween costume — and wear it.

11. Redecorate your room.

12. Create something completely awful and embarrassing —a terrible short story, an over-the-top performance, a disastrous dinner, a fashion don't. (Remember, if you never embarrass yourself or do anything badly, you're not taking any chances!)

13. Keep a journal for at least six months.

> ✂ *LINKS*
> Flip back to Chapter 3 (Write On) for a bunch of creative journal ideas.

14. Throw a costume party — give prizes for the most outrageous outfits.

15. Share your creative talents with others — teach your little brother to play guitar, write a poem for your mom, sing at Grandma's nursing home.

16. Learn how to cook one thing really well, whether it's tacos, bagel pizzas, or duck à l'orange.

> ✂ *LINKS*
> If you're 14 or older, you can have an adventure experience and explore your own abilities by taking a wilderness course with Outward Bound. Check out their Web site at *http://www. outwardbound. org/.*

◆"WRITE IT!" What creative adventures do you want to have before you're 16 (or 18)? List some here.

_____

_____

_____

_____

_____

_____

_____

_____

_____

> "Risk! Risk anything! Care no more for the opinion of others, for those voices. Do the hardest thing on earth for you. Act for yourself. Face the truth."
> — Katherine Mansfield, author

Taking risks

Creativity also involves taking risks — the very essence of adventure. Every time you create something and every time you have any kind of adventure, you're taking some kind of risk, whether it's the risk of embarrassment, a physical risk, or the risk of showing your real thoughts and feelings to other people.

You most often think of risks as being

physical, like breaking your leg or getting eaten by sharks — or getting beaten up by other kids. But there are risks that are emotional, too. I mentioned the risk of embarrassment — that's a big one, and a lot of people, especially adults, don't like to take chances on being creative because they're afraid of being embarrassed. Failing is another risk that lots of people don't like to take. And sharing your true feelings can be scary no matter how old you are.

As freaky as it may be, it's important to take risks in life, because few things of real value are accomplished without risk. Think of a baby learning to walk. Every time she pulls her little body to a standing position and takes a toddling step, she risks falling down. But without the sense of curiosity and adventure that motivates her to take that risk again and again, she'd never learn to walk and, eventually, run.

When you go for an A on a test, you risk failing. When you stand up for yourself, you risk not being taken seriously or losing friends. When you learn to ski, you risk getting hurt or looking stupid. When you create something that has the stamp of your soul on it, you

> "If you're never scared or embarrassed or hurt, it means you never take any chances."
> — Julia Sorel, author

risk baring your heart. But usually anything that's worth having is worth the risk it takes to get it.

✔ *REALITY CHECK* One risk Courtney took? "Telling my family about my depression," she says. "It was one of the hardest things I've ever done because my family is into gossiping. But it was a good risk to take, because I wanted them to know how I truly felt about things."

✏ *WRITE IT!* What's an accomplishment you're proud of?

_____

What kind of risk(s) did you have to take to do this?

_____

_____

_____

_____

As important as it is to take risks, it's also crucial to recognize the difference between a good risk and a bad risk. Filling your life with good risks helps you to grow, and so does avoiding bad risks.

Positive risks are risks you take with a positive goal in mind, like winning a competition or finding new friends. They help you expand your whole self and explore your possibilities. Even when it involves some kind of physical danger, positive risk-taking is done responsibly and can teach you something. So for example, although learning to ski can be dangerous, you can do it carefully and responsibly, and in the process gain a new skill, get fit, *and* learn about the kinds of physical challenges you enjoy.

Negative risks, or dangerous risks, involve putting yourself in some kind of danger without thinking about the consequences — or without caring that there are negative consequences. Taking drugs or stealing are examples of negative risks. They don't help you learn about yourself or gain anything positive. In fact, some negative risk-taking actually makes you less whole, by encouraging you to ignore your values or gut feelings that tell you that something is wrong.

> **⧜*LINKS***
> In *Spirit,* Chapter 2 (What Matters to You — and Why It Matters), we talk more about the values that are important to you and how to stay true to them. *Spirit,* Chapter 3 (The Way You Feel), has more on using your intuition to stay true to yourself. And *Spirit,* Chapter 4 (Choices), talks about putting it all together to make the right decisions that keep you whole — including whether or not to take that risk.

109

Positive risks	Negative risks
have a positive goal	have no particular goal
support your values	go against your values
make you more whole	make you less whole

Go for it!

One thing that deserves another mention in all this talk about adventures and risks: fear. Fear keeps us from taking risks; it holds us back from our adventures.

> "Courage is resistance to fear, mastery of fear — not absence of fear."
> — Mark Twain, author

Fear would rather that we live safe, boring lives than fun, creative ones.

What keeps fear from running the show? Courage and the willingness to go for it. Courage doesn't mean you're never afraid. The bravest people in the world are often afraid. They just go ahead and confront those challenges even when they *are* afraid.

✔ **REALITY CHECK** "My first Speech and Debate competition was really scary," remembers Marianne. "Like a lot of people, I was afraid of speaking in front of people, and the competition was an hour away from home, which didn't help. My mom came with me and watched, which was comforting." To take her mind off her fear, Marianne focused on getting ready for her speech. "I sized up my opponents, did tongue twisters to warm up my mouth, and jumped around to keep my body loose. I knew I looked like a total idiot, but it made me kind of laugh at myself and I hope hid my nervousness."

"I told a guy I liked him," says Amy of a scary moment for her. "Maybe it doesn't sound like a big deal, but it was a huge thing for me to do. Being egged on and encouraged by my friends was what really got me to do it. Even though the guy didn't like me in that way, he's now my absolute best friend, so it all turned out great."

To help get up the courage to go for it, try this:

1. **Take a deep breath.** It'll help calm you down.
2. **Imagine the very worst that could possibly happen.** You trip coming out of the starting

blocks and your humiliating picture is on the front page of the newspaper the next day. You forget every word of your speech, pee in your pants, faint out of embarrassment, and have to be carried to the nurse's office. Now, how likely is it that it actually *will* happen? Pretty unlikely, right?

3. **Imagine the very best that could possibly happen.** You give the most brilliant speech of your lifetime, and children learn your name in school for decades to come. You scale the rock face without making any mistakes. Imagine it over and over again. Walk yourself through it, step-by-step. Fix it in your brain. Won't you feel so proud of yourself when you've done it?

4. **Make sure your parachute straps are secure.** In other words, take all the precautions you need to make yourself feel less nervous. Practice your audition piece, plan what you're going to say when you ask your teacher about that lousy grade, make sure your shoes are tied so you won't trip, tight-

en the straps on your parachute pack. Um, and pee before you go.

5. **Take another deep breath, and do it!**

Of course, sometimes fear is a healthy signal *not* to go ahead. Your body and soul often know what's good for you even when your head doesn't. Humans developed fear as a way to keep us out of real danger. The tricky part is to tell the difference between fear that helps you and fear that holds you back.

Ask yourself, are you afraid of embarrassing yourself, or afraid of something just because it's new or different? Is the thing you're afraid of (like heights, or dogs, or giving oral reports) something that, rationally, you know there's no reason to be this afraid of? Then it could be that your fear is holding you back.

On the other hand, are you afraid of doing something because it's truly dangerous (doing handstands on the edge of your roof, for example, or wandering around alone at night), against your values (stealing), or has negative consequences? Then

> ⚛°*LINKS*
> To read more about fear and other feelings and how to trust your inner signals, turn to *Spirit,* Chapter 3 (The Way You Feel).

113

your fear is probably doing what it's supposed to —
keeping you safe.

WRITE IT! List three activities that totally
scare you.

_____

_____

_____

Do your fears serve a purpose? Is there a safe
way to try any of these activities?

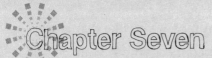

Chapter Seven

Dreaming and Doing

Do you love something?

Caring deeply about something, anything — a person, an idea, a sports team, a band, a book, a hobby — adds color and happiness to your life. Loving something fills you up, expands you, inspires you creatively, gives you focus for your dreams, and energizes the whole you.

> ✓ ***REALITY CHECK*** "I found my favorite band through a guy who went to my school," says Chelsye. "At first I thought the lead singer was a psycho because he made some weird noises, but as soon as I really listened to some other songs of theirs I just fell in love with the music. They've been my favorite band since sixth grade, and they have changed my life dramatically. Just listening to their music has helped me through a lot of rough times. I don't take everything for granted now."

Having something that moves you like that is wonderful. It can connect you to yourself and make you feel more whole. I know that in all the tough times in my life, playing music or writing has helped me get through my troubles and healed me inside. And in the good times, music and writing have helped me celebrate!

LINKS
Friends and Family has lots of tips on healthy ways to connect with the people you love.

Once in a while, though, loving something with all your heart can challenge your sense of wholeness. That can happen if you get so wrapped up in one thing that you forget about everything else. A guy gets so involved with his girlfriend that he blows off school and all his friends; a girl is so into her favorite singer that she stays up all night, every night, building a Web site dedicated to her idol.

LINKS
To read more about balancing your loves and priorities, pick up *Spirit,* Chapter 2 (What Matters to You — and Why It Matters).

To keep the things you love from taking over your life in an unhealthy way, remember to always try to find balance. Balance means making time for different elements in your life, from the stuff you love to the stuff you might not love so much but need to do, like summer reading and visiting your weird aunts and uncles.

✳*WORK IT!* Imagine yourself doing something you love. Draw it.

✐*WRITE IT!* What are some things you love? (Books, bands, creative activities, anything you can think of!)

_____

_____

_____

_____

_____

_____

_____

_____

_____

_____

Dreams and goals

When you get wrapped up in something you totally love, it's fun to dream up dreams related to it. If you love music, maybe you dream about being a rock star or a famous concert pianist. If you fall in love with a book about World War II, maybe you fantasize about what it would be like to live back then, and make up your own stories about it.

Dreaming and imagination are important parts of creativity — it's nearly impossible to be creative without them. I hope this book has helped you dream up crazy stories and visions and performances and let your imagination run wild. Most of the exercises in here are intended to unleash the inspiration you've got inside.

"Dreams are the touchstones of our characters."
— Henry David Thoreau, philosopher and author

But dreaming isn't important only to painting, or writing, or chasing after an adventure. It's also crucial to wholeness. Dreaming about who you want to be and what you want to do encourages you to expand your concept of yourself. Any daydream, no matter how crazy, gives you a glimpse of part of the whole you — the ambition that makes you want to be president, the romanticism that brings fantasies of living in Victorian times, the secret longing for danger that makes you wonder what it would be like to be a stuntman. While not all your dreams may come true, every single one of them helps create the whole you.

✓ *REALITY CHECK* Dreams can be as little or as big as you choose. Sydney wants to have a horse farm. Christina wants to be a house designer. Shauna wants to be a Hollywood director, "and I want to change the world," she adds. Izzy wants to be a chef. Courtney wants to try bungee jumping or skydiving. Marianne says, "I've had all sorts of career aspirations: a zookeeper, a ballerina, an artist like my mom, a lawyer, the president."

Dreaming is a way to use your creativity to create a vision of your own life. There's no right or wrong way to dream — the visions you have are yours alone. Embracing them and letting them take you on their crazy journeys is the best way to begin to construct real goals for your life.

➤*WRITE IT!* Make a list of everything you'd like to do in your life, no matter how crazy, like becoming President, singing on Broadway, taking a helicopter ride, visiting the South Pole, writing a novel, starting your own business, and so on. Dream big!

WORK IT! Make a collage of images and words that represent your wildest, craziest dreams for the future.

WRITE IT! Write a short newspaper article about yourself at age twenty-five. What are you doing? Why are you important enough to have an article about yourself? What do you say in the interview?

WORK IT! Imagine that you're famous. Make a fake magazine cover with your face on it, and write cover lines about who you are and why you're featured on a magazine. You can do this using cutouts and collages, or if you're technically savvy, scan your picture and create the cover on your computer.

WRITE IT! Pick one of your biggest dreams. Write a story or play in which you imagine yourself fulfilling that dream. (If you prefer, create a painting or a film instead.)

Making it happen

Some dreams are just for fun, but just about any dream can come true if you really want it to. Setting concrete goals for yourself is a way of making dreams come true. When you set a goal and work toward achieving it, you create a focus around which you can organize yourself and your life. Hopefully that goal is consistent with who you are or who you want to be; that way it helps keep you whole, too.

Turning a dream into a goal and then into a reality can seem like an impossibly huge task sometimes. But if you break it down into little parts, it will seem much more manageable. This works whether you're wrestling with a huge, far-off dream (like being a famous movie star) or a smaller, short-term goal (like being cast in the school play).

> **"Dreams come true; without that possibility, nature would not incite us to have them."**
> — John Updike, author

1. **Give your dream a quick true-to-you test.** Before you get started, make sure that this dream is true

✣ *LINKS*
For more on making choices that are true to you, turn to *Spirit,* Chapter 2 (What Matters to You — and Why It Matters), and *Spirit,* Chapter 4 (Choices).

to your values and your vision of yourself. If the whole point of the dream is to change part of your vision of yourself (say, if you're super-shy but you want to be an actress), that's okay — but think really hard about whether this change will require you to turn your back on your most essential self.

2. **Break it into concrete steps.** Next, come up with mini-goals along the path to your dream. If your lifelong dream is to sing on Broadway, some of those mini-goals might be to improve and strengthen your singing voice; try out for your school musical; enroll in a musical theater program; or perform in local productions.

3. **Break down each step even further.** For example, take the mini-goal of improving and strengthening your singing voice. Steps you can take toward that might include taking singing lessons or joining the school chorus or another singing group so you can practice as much as possible. Break those steps down even further — to take singing lessons, you might ask around to

see if anyone knows a good teacher, research how much it costs, figure out how to pay for it (will your parents chip in? do you need to do extra baby-sitting to earn the cash?), and sign up for your first lesson. Keep going until you've broken down the first mini-goal enough that each step seems manageable.

4. **Get started!** Take that first baby step. When that's done, take another. Keep going until you reach your goal!

✔ ***REALITY CHECK*** When Amy started running for the first time in her life, she set herself a goal of being able to run five miles. "Every day, I would run just a little bit farther — I kept practicing and practicing," she says. "By the end of the summer, I was going on a 5.4-mile run every morning, *and* a three-mile jog at night."

Her new goal is to maintain a good grade in her English class. "I did badly last year, but this year I really like my teacher and I'm hoping to do well."

✳️ *WORK IT!* Think of a short-term goal you have, like writing a great article for your school paper or being first chair in band. Using the directions above, create a step-by-step plan to reach that goal.

✒️ *WRITE IT!* Check out the list you made earlier in the chapter of all the things you want to do in your life. Pick one that's really big. List three tiny things you can do right now to get closer to that dream.

_____

_____

_____

Changing dreams

Like many other things about you, your dreams and goals can change and evolve over time. You might have had dreams in the past that no longer feel right to you now, and maybe in the future you'll find new dreams and goals that you can't even imagine today.

✓ *REALITY CHECK* Chelsye says, "My first ever goal was to be famous — I wanted to be in a band so bad. Now, I want to publish a successful novel and, hopefully, with the money from that start my own clothing line."

"I used to want to be rich — I think everyone did," says Marianne. "Now, I want to find a way that I can benefit others. I really want to make a contribution to society, and I think making a difference will be more satisfying than making a lot of money."

It's okay to leave a dream behind if it no longer fits with who you are. If you do decide to abandon a dream or goal, though, I hope it's because it truly doesn't fit with the direction the whole you is taking — and not because it's too hard or because other people think it's weird.

It's nice to remember those old dreams, if only to remind yourself of how crazy creative your dreams can be. And don't forget — those old dreams are still tucked away in a corner of the whole you. Even if they never came true, they made you who you are today.

✳ *WORK IT!* Make a "dream book." Decorate a notebook with pictures that represent your dreams and desires. List all your dreams and goals, no matter how big, small, or crazy. If you want, outline how you plan to make those dreams come true. Keep updating it as your dreams evolve, and use it to remind yourself of your priorities.

✄ *LINKS*
Turn to the section on journals in Chapter 3 (Write On) for more on keeping a journal that's special to you. To read about balancing your priorities and keeping them up-front, read *Spirit*, Chapter 2 (What Matters to You — and Why It Matters).

Creating the Whole You

Live joyfully!

To me, being creative and open to inspiration is a big part of what I like to call living joyfully. Living joyfully doesn't mean you're happy every second of every day — let's face it, that's just not possible. What it means is taking pleasure in life, savoring the good moments as much as possible, finding the joy in even dark moments when you can, and just generally living life to the fullest.

When you're in tune with your creative spirit, whether that means writing a poem, inventing an adventure, or dreaming of being President, you're hooking up with the joy in your life.

WRITE IT! When was the last time you felt totally happy? Where were you? What were you doing? Describe it in detail.

Feeling fulfilled

The more joyfully you live, the more fulfilled you feel in your everyday life. Being *fulfilled* is something that grown-ups talk about a lot, but what it basically

127

means here is *filling yourself up,* or filling up the whole you. Exploring your hopes, desires, and creative dreams — and feeling like you're doing all you can to fulfill them — is an important part of nurturing your wholeness. If you don't feel fulfilled, you're not whole.

Part of feeling fulfilled is feeling like you're doing something important. That doesn't necessarily mean that it's important to the world or important to your teachers or parents — it means something that's important to YOU. Indulging your creative nature is important; so is following your dreams.

It's all inside you

Finding creative inspiration and fulfillment is up to you. You've got the resources within yourself — your imagination, ideas, and the unique way you see the world — to make every day a creative masterpiece! I hope this book has inspired you to connect with your inner creativity. To continue exploring your creative potential, keep your creative juices flowing by tapping into them, just a little bit, every day.

☀ *WORK IT!* Make a "creativity lotto" so you'll be sure to flex your creative muscles every

day. On slips of paper, write different quick creative activities. You can pick activities from the
rest of this book, use the suggestions below,
or invent your own. (Coming up with them is a
creativity exercise itself!)

Some suggested lotto activities:
- Make up new words to your favorite song.
- With your eyes closed, draw a picture of
  yourself.
- Decorate old jars, take-out containers, or
  plastic storage boxes and use them to
  hold pencils, coins, and other random
  stuff.
- Stand on your head. (You can prop yourself up against a wall!)
- Make hats for your pets.
- Discover what your voice sounds like
  when you sing in different positions —
  lying flat on the floor, hanging your head
  off the bed, curled up in a ball, or standing on your toes reaching for the ceiling.
- Paint each of your fingernails a different
  color.

- Bake cookies.
- Get out the blocks or Legos you played with as a little kid. Build a fantastical city.
- Teach yourself to wiggle your ears.
- Stage an enormous battle involving every toy, stuffed animal, and doll in your house. At the end, declare a truce.
- Wear your pajamas inside out and backward.
- Write a poem.
- Try to come up with at least thirty or forty different activities. Put all the slips of paper into a box or jar — be sure to decorate it! Draw a different one each day, and follow the instructions.

"Imagination is more important than knowledge."
— Albert Einstein, physicist

Dig deep into your creative spirit, and never be afraid to dream up new hopes and ideas. You've got a whole lifetime of creative adventure ahead of you — and a million unique ways to express THE WHOLE YOU.

Books to Indulge
Your Creativity

In no particular order, here are a bunch of books for more creative ideas, activities, and inspiration.

A Book of Artrageous Projects (Klutz Inc., 2000) — Tons of fun art projects that you can do right in the book, from painting, drawing, and collage to metalwork and stained glass.

A Blank Journal: For Teens and Beyond (Klutz Inc., 1999)

My Life According to Me (Klutz Inc., 1999) — A twist on the blank book theme, these journals come with black pages and a silver pen. The first has a handy envelope at the back to keep photos and other memorabilia, the second has quizzes and games for when you just don't know what to write.

Dream Journal (Klutz Inc., 2000) — Exactly what the name says . . .

The Art Book (Phaidon Press Inc., 1997) — A guide to the world's greatest painters and sculptors, with lots of illustrations of their work.

The Story of the Orchestra, by Robert Levine (Black Dog & Leventhal, 2001) — A guide to classical composers and their musical periods, plus the instruments of the orchestra. Comes with a CD of musical selections you can listen to with the book.

Eyewitness Books: Music, by Neil Ardley (Dorling Kindersley, 2000) — A photographic guide to musical instruments (including zithers, electric guitars, and more), plus explanations of how they work.

The Book of Rhythms, by Langston Hughes (Oxford University Press, 2000) — The famous poet talks about rhythm and all the ways it's a part of our lives.

Break a Leg! The Kids' Guide to Acting and Stagecraft, by Lisa Friedman (Workman, 2002)

The Skit Book: 101 Skits from Kids, by Margaret Read MacDonald (Linnet Books, 1990)

Girl Director: A How-to Guide for the First-time, Flat-broke Film & Video Maker, by Andrea Richards (Girl Press, 2001) — Not just for girls!

The Young Writer's Companion, by Sarah Ellis (Groundwood Books, 1999)

Hey, Day! by Super Clea and Keva Marie (Harper-Trophy, 2001) — 365 days of fun activities.

The Ultimate Book of Kid Concoctions, by John E. Thomas and Danita Pagel (Kid Concoctions Co., 1998) — Make all kinds of goops, potions, and paints with random stuff around your house.

Making Books That Fly, Fold, Wrap, Hide, Pop Up, Twist, and Turn, by Gwen Diehn (Lark Books, 1998)

Simple Sewing (Klutz Inc., 1999)

Beadlings: How to Make Beaded Creatures and Creations, by Julie Collings and Candice Elton (Klutz Inc., 2000)

The Fannie Farmer Junior Cookbook, by Joan Scobey (Little Brown, 2000)

The New Way Things Work, by David Macauley (Houghton Mifflin, 1998)

Appendix B
Research Resources

These Web sites can help you in your quest to explore your curiosity. Note: All sites were working at press time; however, I can't guarantee they'll still be up.

At **Ask Jeeves Kids,** just type in a question and Jeeves will find the answer. Try it at **http://www.ajkids.com/** Check out **Britannica.com (http://www.britannica. com/)** to look stuff up in the Encyclopaedia Britannica.

Encarta.com (http://encarta.msn.com) has an on-line encyclopedia, dictionary, and atlas, plus homework help when you need it.

KidsClick! is a directory put together by librarians to help kids find cool Web sites. It includes news sites, the arts, health, science, geography, and tons more. Go to **http://sunsite.berkeley.edu/KidsClick!/**

The New York Times Student Connections site has news, puzzles, news quizzes, and other cool resources. Find it at **http://www.nytimes.com/learning/students**

The Yuckiest Site on the Internet (http://yucky.kids. discovery.com/) has info on all things gross, slimy, and disgusting, from worms and roaches to cool, gross stuff about your body.

Recommended Reading

If you'd like to further explore some of the themes in this book, here are some books you might want to check out. They deal with the arts and all sorts of other creative concepts, and, of course, they're all great reads, too.

Weetzie Bat, by Francesca Lia Block

Alice's Adventures in Wonderland, by Lewis Carroll

King of Shadows, by Susan Cooper

Love That Dog, by Sharon Creech

Charlie and the Chocolate Factory, by Roald Dahl

The Man in the Ceiling, by Jules Feiffer

Yolonda's Genius, by Carol Fenner

The Phantom Tollbooth, by Norton Juster

From the Mixed-up Files of Mrs. Basil E. Frankweiler, by E. L. Konigsberg

The Chronicles of Narnia, by C. S. Lewis

Emily of New Moon, by L. M. Montgomery

A Light in the Attic, by Shel Silverstein

Dancing Shoes, by Noel Streatfeild

The Mozart Season, by Virginia Euwer Wolf

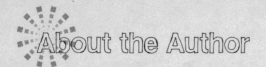

About the Author

Jeannie Kim is a former editor and writer for *YM* and *Twist*. She's written about everything from fortune-tellers to snack foods to incredibly embarrassing moments. Her work has also appeared in *CosmoGIRL!*, *Your Prom*, and TigerBeat.com, as well as in many magazines for adults. When she's not writing, she can be found playing the electric violin onstage with a rock band or laying down tracks in the studio. She was born and raised in Wisconsin but somehow found her way to New York City, where she now lives with her husband and their cat, Deirdre.